Dear Jay, Freya and Meadow,

I hope one day you will be able to read this book. I hope you will be able to bare the pain within its pages. I hope you'll come to know the truth about how you were loved, wanted, and fought for.

I'm not perfect; these words will tell you that. But I'm also not what I have been demonised to be by a billion-pound industry that quite literally deals in the exchange of kids for cash.

I can't change what's happened, but I fought hard to stop it. I can't undo the time missed, but I am here going forward.

I would not have been able to take you on holidays around the world, bought us a big house, put you in branded clothing and given you opportunities to do all the amazing things you have done with your adoptive parents. I didn't and still don't have that kind of money. I'm working class, I am not high powered, rich, or well-travelled. I am quite unextraordinary.

But I would have loved you. I'd have cared for you, advocated for you when school got tough, caught the train to the seaside for ice cream and 2p machines. I'd have taken you on barefoot walks in the forest and educated you in identifying edible foods and played splash in muddy puddles.

I may not have been the mother who would give you all the material things you deserve but I'd have given you that which matters, love, loyalty, time, security, roots and wisdom. Unfortunately, the circumstances did not allow that at the time. With a heavy heart, here's the story of why you were denied the love of your birth family.

Dedicated to justice, who has been denied her right to reign for too long

Authors note

I'd like to start by thanking you for taking the time to read this book and being open to hearing my experience rather than making assumptions.

I am not a professional writer, and I am self-publishing. I cannot promise there will not be typos however please do not let this takeaway from the validity of my words. This is my story, as full as I can tell it.

This key below may be helpful as I use some abbreviations throughout this text.

LA – Local Authority
FGC – Family group conference
BPD – borderline personality disorder
SCBU – special care baby unit
CPR- child protection register
CPTSD – complex post-traumatic stress disorder

Forced adoption is the term used to describe the act of social services and the family courts, removing infants from their biological families, and placing them for **permanent** adoption, against the parents' wishes. Concerns such as *'possible emotional harm'* are often used to justify this life altering action. In the case of forced adoption, the birth parents, do not *'give up'* their child. They do not consent to the adoption.

You may be reading this as a birth parent, adopter, or adoptee. Maybe a law professional or social worker. This book is not intended to speak on behalf of any group or cause offence to these groups. This book is based on my experience with the local authority and courts. **It is not a source intended to offer legal advice or any kind of assistance for any given group.**

All names and places or other identifying information have been changed for legal and confidentiality purposes, including my own.

This book is simply one birth mother coming forward to finally share her tragic experience within the family court justice system in the UK. This corrupt process is causing a pandemic of adoption trauma across the globe.
Please keep an open mind. There will be things that will challenge your perspective. Even I can't believe some of the things that occurred.

Introduction

Adoption is often not the fairy tale that society has sold you. It is often trauma, more for the child and its birth parents than anyone else. Yet, after an adoption, did you know it's the adopting party who get counselling and support? Why? They have everything they wanted to complete their family, right? What did the birth parents get left with but an empty womb and heart?

Adoption is a billion-pound industry across the globe with the wealthier of our society paying out their cash to complete their family ideals. Adoption is not just a cash cow but a lair of lies and a menagerie of manipulation, trafficking off infants to the highest bidder.

It's not always about helping a poor unwanted orphan. A lot of the time, a child up for adoption has in fact been stolen under forced adoption laws. This is me and my family's story, as well as that of many other families across our world.

This is a story that's taken me 16 years to begin sharing thanks to the lasting psychological devastation the local authority (LA) caused and the stigma attached of being a 'birth mum.'

Adoptees still get abused and neglected by these so-called heroic adopters. Adoptees still grow up feeling overwhelmed with feelings they cannot name or are simply forbidden to discuss. A primal wound they can't even remember receiving.

Empty mothers wander without direction just hoping to find their child's face in every crowd, while an oblivious person or persons raise the stolen child, often believing they are doing god's good work. Oh my, how as a social structure we have been fooled.

Adoption does not promise a better life, just a different one. It splits timelines and rips open wounds that will never heal because the never knowing does not seal itself. It is eternal. Unlived lives we never get back. Adoption is all what ifs and wonderings.

Many people say, 'adoption is beautiful,' and it is, for the adopters. These hopeful parents will say 'this child completes our family,' but they'll never admit it came at the expense of another family. They may even be quick to tell you how they paid thousands of pounds for the child, to an agency, never donating to causes that help parents in poverty keep their child. Poverty often being considered neglect and cause for the LA to remove a child.

After a traumatic life, just a few weeks shy of 18, I birthed my son into this world. My earliest memory of being a mum is being too tired to hold my baby. A guilt I carried for years because I naively believed mothering was a natural phenomenon that I'd suddenly develop once a baby came out of me.

If any first-time mummies are reading this, please know, not everyone adapts to motherhood instantly. It's ok to be scared and confused. I wish someone had told me that back then.

My second pregnancy was planned. This pregnancy should have been a joyful family experience, and it became anything but.

I kept having a reoccurring dream that would leave me jolting awake, covered in sweat, and feeling panicked. The same dream of a tiger and hyenas hunted me many nights. I'd dream they were prowling around outside my home, looking up at me as I peeped from behind the curtains. Sometimes they would be on the local recreation ground, lurking and waiting for me as I walked to town.

It took me until writing this book to realise, that was my intuition telling me something. Because opposite that rec ground was the LA office; the very home of the animals preying upon me.

Something felt off from the start. Throughout the entire pregnancy I kept saying someone was stalking me and waiting to steal my baby when it was born. Words like 'paranoid' and 'delusional' were used and my use of cannabis blamed. You'd be forgiven for being agreeable to those assessments but here's the real kicker; I wasn't wrong, was I......

To My First-Born Son

You are beautiful
you are free
you are everything to me.
Whether near
or whether far
I am proud of who you are.
You are love
you are divine
you are everything that's kind.
Whether kin
or whether guest
To know you I am blessed.
You are salvation
you are solution
you are everything that's revolution.
Whether hushed
whether roaring
your purpose is worth exploring.
And as I love you
I beg, love yourself too
for there is nothing more divinely precious than you

Chapter one

He is pink in the cheeks and red eyed. His greasy dark hair is glued to his sweaty face. He clearly had a wine at lunch. No, not my husband, the social worker, Callum. You can expect West, my husband, to be drunk by noon but he's not in work or interfering in others' lives for a living.

I'm trying to convey to this man how frustrated I am by West's drinking. Anyone can see he has an issue and it's affecting us all. But this man's only response is that West deserves a few beers at the end of the day when our son is asleep. I add that it's a lot more than a few and he swiftly moves on to me. After all, I'm always the problem.

How's my mental health? What did the psychiatrist say at my latest visit? I answered honestly. Out of nowhere Callum decided that West and Jay should go stay in the city with West's mother. It was very sudden and unexpected, but West was more than happy to shoot off for what he perceived as a holiday with our child and leave me behind. This was not the first time I would have been kept from my son because West and me were having an issue.

I asked how long this would be for and Callum replied, 'until you learn to behave yourself little girl.' He was belittling me instead of justifying the action he was taking to split a family a part.

I was deeply confused and quickly begun to rage. I could feel my brain crumbling under the pressure of trying to comprehend what was happening.

West started shoving things into carrier bags while Callum attempted to put Jay in his pushchair. I tried to stop them leaving but Callum pushed me aside and rammed the pushchair into my shins, so I moved.

As I stood on the doorstep screaming and totally overwhelmed by the sudden turn of events, I could see Jay twisting in his pushchair, his little hand out like a star, shouting 'mummy,' over and over and Callum literally grabbing Jay's head and turning it away from me.

I ended up in A&E later that day having taken myself there as I was anxious and not feeling strong mentally. Given I had now been unmedicated for 7 months and left to cope alone, it was fair to say I was in a bad way with depression at this point and now I was totally alone and expecting a baby with a man who just walked out on me, with my son, after having what you'd consider a normal day in our married life.

Literally nothing had been wrong that day, not until Callum turned up. But now I suddenly felt like I was crazy and worthless and I had been abandoned, again, triggering deep pains from my childhood.

I was discharged after a quick chat with the on-call psych. There wasn't any immediate risk, and I was otherwise healthy. They got me in a taxi and sent me off with the assurance I was perfectly fine and going to be fine going forward.

24 hours later, I was being admitted to a psych ward against my will. That was the start of what would become a lengthily battle to keep custody of my children.

That first night alone was hell. Laying there in my sons abandoned bed I had every light on in the house. Every knock and bump had me on edge. I was utterly alone except the eerie feeling that often haunted me in that house, lingering like a shawl over my shoulders. But after a little sleep, I woke and got straight into my day.

I was not speaking to any family at all at that point, so I didn't bother to call anyone to update them or ask for help. Truth is, once Jay had been big enough to sit up and not sleep adorably in people's arms, nobody came to visit anymore. They quickly tired of the new baby. After the first few months, the visits dwindled rapidly down to nothing.

Me and 2 of my family members had, had an argument before xmas. They'd come over to give Jay his gifts and to spend some time with him. For some reason they had arrived in a foul mood.

The energy of the room shifted when they arrived and even Jay was quiet to start. You could just see there was something up, but me and West decided not to ask questions, assuming they'd argued in the car.

Jay was playing with his new toys, and we were all chatting as we'd not seen one another in a while. They asked about our elderly neighbour, and we said he was home from the hospital, having had a heart attack a few months before. I remarked how we'd been sent a xmas card that year which had surprised me as it was clear the neighbours didn't really like us. At this, one family member decided it was the perfect opening to get her show on the road.

I was snapped at immediately *'well you should have sent one back you horrible girl.'*

West quickly jumped to my defence. *"Excuse me!"* He was stunned beyond those words and I was fuming.

"FOR YOUR INFORMATION WE DID SEND ONE BACK BUT YOU DIDN'T LET ME FINISH DID YOU!" and I left the room and went upstairs with the intention of staying there until they left, avoiding further arguments. It was clear after all, they were there to see Jay, not me.

They were already out the front door by the time I got upstairs. They could not wait to leave. They hardly even said goodbye to Jay who was a little perplexed by the sudden departure.

I didn't speak to either of these people again until early spring when I arrived in the psych ward. I never really bought the subject up, having bigger things to worry about by the time our reunion came. But it did transpire, sometime later, the situation didn't go

11

'unpunished.' The reason social services came to our door the first day in the new year, was because, both mine and West's family talked about us and plotted to call the LA. They later said they were concerned and trying to get us 'help' but it remains clear to this day, it was out of spite! These people were always class A manipulative and abusive and together they were a deadly combo.

No doubt they hadn't expect it to go as far as it did. But the worst part of this sorry family tale is that one of them, years later, would be the one to pressure me into getting sterilised because *'the family don't need all that pain and loss again we've suffered enough.'*

Fast forward some weeks later from that event and my world was collapsing under the sudden revival of the LA in my life. However, without West there, I felt refreshed and new. I blitzed half the house. The washing machine broke down and instead of crying I filled the bathtub and washed things by hand. I was already coming round to the idea of just me and the baby. I didn't smoke cannabis at all that day, and I was perfectly settled most of the time, except when trying to call my mother-in-law to speak to my son, which she forbid.

Then later that evening a pair of doctors and social worker who I had never met turned up on my doorstep. A midwife attended also and claimed I had left a voicemail the previous night threatening to kill myself and the baby.

I said I had called midwifery before heading to A&E and explained my distress. I tried to tell them what I had actually been trying to convey and that I was concerned how being unmedicated for quite some time was having a toll on my ability to function and that I was now alone and concerned for my mental state. I was open about feeling suicidal and depressed and how I felt afraid at night.

12

I recall crying, barely able to breathe as I hurled the words out through wracking sobs. I was desperate to convey I wanted help and someone to advocate for me.

I elaborated further how the psychiatrist I had been working with was also pregnant, due around the same time and I felt she was not able to detach her personal feelings. I was trying to say I felt the cons of medication in pregnancy had been weighed wrong. Afterall, she kept telling me she would not risk exposing her baby to medications.

Just into my third Trimester, this doctor did prescribe me some kind of antidepressant. On day 2 I vomited. It had been a few months since morning sickness wore off, but I had taken to vomiting later into pregnancy with Jay also. But West felt it was my body rejecting the drugs because of the baby. He agreed with the psychiatrist and reminded me he was the baby's dad, and he had a say. I stopped taking them.

I'm sure my message would have been alarming and most certainly needed to be followed up and not put down to hormonal hysterics. So, 48 hours later, here we were, all squished into the tiny sitting room. Four unfamiliar figures towering over me.

I said I'd been assessed and sent home and asked them why, if I was such a danger to the baby, wasn't someone sent out immediately? Why wait almost 2 days?

I raised this again in court, no one ever answered. Nor were they ever able to provide this recorded voicemail for the court. A voicemail they claimed was a serious indication I was planning to harm my unborn baby.

For such a serious allegation, you'd think hearsay would be inadequate, I mean this was an unborn babies' life. In a society that values the foetus more than the mother, you'd think action would be immediate.

I was made to go to the local psychiatric ward. I was threatened and told if I did not go willingly, I'd be 'fully sectioned' and must stay for a minimum of 6 months. But if I went now, I'd be able to prove I was ok and come home. This was the start of some extensive manipulation.

On my arrival I was not given an assessment or induction interview or taken through any official admission procedure. I was just taken to my room. I was never invited for meetings, assessments or asked to take the wellness surveys all other patients were given to monitor their health. My stay there was a highly unusual circumstance.

I spent about 8 weeks in that ward. I was scared and kept from my son that whole time. I was not allowed to attend meetings about my son or unborn baby, I was forbidden to speak to my husband, still denied medication and therapy during my stay and every time I tried to go home or ask too many questions I'd be told 'you will be fully sectioned if you leave, you'll be here a minimum of 6 months.' Yet I could go for walks or even into town. I was such a risk, but I could go anywhere, just not home. It was all very confusing.

This constant state of confusion and isolation causes tension and stress. When we feel trapped and no one tells us why we are trapped, we are traumatised by it. We become hostile and untrusting; doesn't sound like the sort of relationship a social worker or doctor should be developing with a parent they claim they want to work with for the kids best interest.

Consider how mental health issues shot through the roof during the Covid lockdowns. That's a fine example of why isolation is damaging to us as humans.

Chapter Two

During my stay I was sexually assaulted, flashed at and stolen from by another female patient. It was all hushed up and they told me I couldn't press charges even though they had seen her and had to restrain her. Sexual assault is not because of mental illness. I remain effected by that incident to this day.

I expressed that I felt me, and my baby were no longer safe, and I was going home. I was threatened again with my extended stay.

The next day Callum visited and wanted me to sign some papers. It should have rung alarm bells. No one sectioned or being held against their will due to being mentally unstable should be expected to sign legal contracts, especially with no lawyer present.

The room was bright and glaring and it reflected violently off his slicked back, gunky dark hair, a strand of which hung around his blood shot eyes. The pure white top I was wearing clashed against everything else in the room and I suddenly realised how big I was getting.

He hands me some papers and a pen. Callum explains he now sees what I mean about my husband's drinking and to protect my son and the baby when it's born, I needed to sign this form so he could *'do what he can to help out.'* He manipulated me with my current dislike for West,

a dislike he had largely caused.

Unbeknown to me until years later, this form agreed to have my kids placed with adopters. I had signed my kids away believing this social worker was finally going to help me get rehomed and away from West, who was, quite frankly, an alcoholic and emotional abuser.

He told me he'd visit West and Jay in the city and keep me informed. I never heard from him again, until the day after baby 2 was born.

To this day, what I still don't understand is, if this form allowed them to take both children into care (I later found it was a section 21) why was Jay left with West for several more weeks but the baby to be born would be removed within hours?

I had just finished dinner. A decent beef stroganoff was had, sat with Luke and Anne, 2 older patients. We had been giggling about me selecting curry for dinner the following evening in the attempt to get me into labour.

We sat by the open window, enjoying the warmth of the sun and colliding coolness of the April breeze. It was a great end to the day. I never thought that within 6 hours, I'd be the most depressed I'd ever been.

 I was walking to my room when I felt my waters go. Three hours later my daughter, Freya, arrived. A beautiful water birth accompanied by my mother and grandmother, not a man in sight, except the police officer I could see standing outside the door because the social workers had told the midwives I may try to take the baby.

The birth was an incredible experience that replays in my brain frequently, even though this ethereal memory ends with permanent pain.

I felt the emptiness as Freya left my vessel and was now amidst the water that was turning to a red ocean. The midwife struggled to find her to bring to the surface, the blood obscuring the bottom of the pool.

Eventually Freya is placed unharmed into my arms. "Hi, mummy has waited so long to meet you." In that moment it was just me and her, everything else faded out for just a few sweet seconds while I marvelled at this tiny life I had bought into the world. I was bleeding a lot, so I was popped onto the bed with Freya placed on my chest.

I had wanted to deliver the placenta naturally and no matter how much tugging the midwife did, it was not willing to depart so I accepted the injection. The bleed was seemingly nothing to be concerned about, even though I was whiter than snow for many weeks to come and so I used this hour to my advantage and immersed myself with my child.

But even at this stage, because I'd not been allowed to attend any meetings or communicate with West, I had no idea Freya was being taken from me. I didn't know until I gave birth. That's how long I was lied to. Can you imagine the damage that confusion does to a woman and a baby?

I hadn't been unwell for the whole 8 weeks I had been there. No bad behaviour. No obvious depression or angry outburst, except when I was told I could not attend meetings about my son. It was almost as if the problem was gone.

There was no need to put police in eyeshot. I wasn't a hardened criminal or dangerous mental patient; I was a human being trying to give birth. Seeing the other parents faces as I waddled up the corridor was mortifying.

Three hours after Freya made her way into the big world my birth partners went home and me and Freya were alone. Within 2 minutes a midwife came and without looking up from her feet, explained she'd have to take the baby and someone was here to take me back across to my ward.

I never forget the way her voice shook with shame, the expendable messenger who clearly didn't sign up for this. She wheeled my baby out the room to the special care unit. There is no silence more deafening, than the one left behind, as they wheel the crib away.

The day is warm and bright. I sit in my chair, feet up on the side of the bed and a Harry Potter book atop of my absurdly protruding abdomen. I've re-read the series whilst here, reading aloud for the baby to hear because I read it can hear the outside world and exposing it to language in utero can benefit their brain development. My abdomen ripples, jutting the book up and down like a sailboat at sea. I lower the book to have this moment of interaction with my unborn child.

My hands follow the flow as she manoeuvres herself about in her cramped home, when suddenly a tiny foot appears in the taut skin. I can see a defined point of a heel and several tiny toes, almost as if the veil between me and the child was lifted.

I let out a tiny yelp of shock. The reality that an entire human is wriggling around in my womb suddenly occurs to me and I realise the magnitude of that; just how incredible life is. Life I am creating.

The Harry Potter book resting upon my swollen belly doesn't even compare to the absolute magic of my offspring rolling over within me and rippling my abdomen like a blanket.

I poke the tiny apparition and its quickly retracted much to my amusement. All stills and I return to the magical world of Hogwarts.

Spit the truth and watch it cascade from their faces,
be the roar that shakes the skin from their bones.
Never be silent in the face of adversity,
allow azure fires to flay your tongue, ready to burn the
foundations.
Let the tap of fingers on keys be the marching anthem,
to the trenches of the soul.

I go with nothing but words as my weapon.
They may have won many battles
but they have not won my war.

Chapter Three

The next day I get a supervised visit on SCBU with a random supervisor for one hour. We were crammed in among all those worried parents and sick babies with my healthy baby. An insult to us all.

Another day or so passes and Callum brings the baby to me for a visit. We are bundled into a small office just off the psych ward. He explains how I won't be able to breastfeed the baby. I cry my eyes out the whole hour because I don't understand why. I'm still medication free and she'll be home soon. He had the decency to look ashamed and asked me not to shoot the messenger, as he was only relaying what he'd been asked by his manager.

Still, no one was explaining the LA's intention to take the child into care. I carry on thinking I can have her back when I'm discharged. They left me ignorant so I could not take action to fight. We literally had no idea an adoption would occur until court came because we were led to believe 'reunification and family preservation is the goal.'

I'm released later that day. Less than a handful of days after birth when I've supposedly been a huge risk to myself. I'm sent to live with my grandparents as I'm now homeless. The family home was never in my name, and I currently had no child in my care, so I was not entitled to it, but Callum promised they'd get a flat sorted for me ASAP.

Despite this, West had also been told he couldn't go back to the house either as I may turn up and 'cause problems.' He was told by social workers to give up the house and he did. He and my son were also officially homeless.

Because he had surrendered a council house, he was not entitled to the councils help in getting another one. Very convenient of them not to mention that before he handed it back and made himself voluntarily homeless.

During the first week of Freya's life, she was left alone in a SCBU crib. Being healthy meant she would have only been tended to during feeds and nappy changes and she had been allowed 2 visits from us in total.
 Instead of letting me stay on the ward with her or putting her straight into a foster home or with a family member, they chose to leave a new born alone in a place she didn't need to be.
 The first week of her life she would have been subjected to isolation and emotional neglect. There was zero good reason for this. They had planned on taking my baby for weeks before she was born, a home should have been waiting. After all, the LA love to 'parallel plan,' and I'll discuss this more later.
 I can't imagine what damage this has caused my child. It is scientifically proven that infants being separated from their mother at birth suffer trauma and consequences that can last a lifetime including attachment disorder, anxiety and learning difficulties.
 We don't even remove animals from their mothers for the first few months of life but it's ok for authorities take human babies and leave them laying there like that despite having loving parents sat a few corridors away. That ward was supervised 24/7, I should have been able to visit whenever I liked.

I now get to see my children once a week, at a contact centre. I swear every time they bring Freya they bring a different child. She changes so quickly I doubt I'd have suspected a damn thing if they had bought me the wrong baby. Me and my poor child were strangers to one another.
West and Jay must travel by train to come for these visits and as time goes on and the summer gets warmer, it becomes more taxing

on Jay. He often arrives red faced and grouchy and I don't blame him.

For 8 weeks me and Jay were denied contact and when I first saw him again, he was a different child. He spoke in a monotone voice and didn't smile or seem expressive during interaction. He seemed depressed. Even when he first saw me and was walking towards me with his arms out to cuddle me, he seemed like a zombie. It was heart breaking and I blamed myself for getting locked away. I figured he must hate me.

Freya just cries a lot. Almost all my early contacts consist of her crying the whole time. Refusing the bottle, not needing anything, just both of us in tears with the supervisor, Ursula, tutting, and scribbling notes the whole time.

Apparently, Freya was distressed by my distress. Distress likely caused by all the upheaval we'd both been suffering. But the LA made it purely about me. They even informed me *'she doesn't do this for the foster carer or West, just you.'* Leaving me feeling inadequate and thinking my own baby hated me for a separation I had not chosen.

Most contacts go without any major issues and me and West are kept distant from one another during crossover time to minimise any arguments.

On one occasion we have to swap children. I'm taking Freya and West is collecting Jay. On this occasion we have a quick chat with Callum, so we all end in a room together.

I have a quiet word with Callum about a concern I had with Jay and someone should chat to West. He insisted it was ok for me and West to discuss it ourselves as we were both mature adults. So, I did.

I approached West as softly and discreetly as I could as the kids were still there. He was hostile from the get-go.

I explained that Jay's brain was like a sponge and that he picks up on everything and to maybe ask his brother or whoever helps look after him, to be mindful. He asked me to elaborate so I did. For my son's privacy I will not elaborate here in this book.

West blew up instantly, accused me of accusing his family of abuse, told me I was deluded for thinking my son would behave that way and that I was looking for trouble. I could smell vodka. I instantly held up my hands in surrender and said sorry let's forget it. Callum was smiling in the corner as West slammed Jay into his pushchair and stormed off.

To this day I am sure my concerns were fair and just, especially given West's brother was convicted of exactly what I was concerned my son was exposed too but no one wanted to listen at the time. I was dismissed as paranoid, deluded and dramatic as always.

Another incident that boiled my blood was Freya's vaccinations. I was never asked about my preference, they just went ahead and booked it. I would have consented, and I'd have appreciated the right to have a choice but it seemed I had no choices anymore.

The appointment was set and I was due to meet Freya's foster carer at the surgery. My mum got me there 15 minutes early to make sure we didn't miss it. No sooner had I stepped on the hot tarmac of the car park, the woman I knew to be the foster carer was pushing a pram out of the surgery.

I approached smiling and said hello and was greeted with zero smile and a look of fear. She explained the doctor changed the appointment time that morning and a social worker was supposed to inform me. No one had contacted me and now I had missed my baby's appointment which was later used to criticise me.

I then had to stand there and watch a stranger walk away with my baby, having not even been allowed to give her a kiss because no social worker was present.

After a few weeks West's mum, Sally, decided he and Jay are no longer welcome and must move out. Social services place them in a B&B, in the town where I am now living in my new flat. They did follow through on that, although as a result, I was immediately dropped from mental health services due to there being a change of location. The new local team didn't feel I was mentally ill or needed medicating. So, my only support was gone but I was not fussed. I mean, the social worker got me this flat, Callum wants to help me, right? I genuinely believed this was the result of those papers I'd signed, and I'd be getting my kids back soon. However, I attempted to get re-referred in the hopes I could show the LA I had support going forward with my mental health. I was declined over and over until 2015, way after my kids adoption.

West was struggling. He calls me and arranges to meet me secretly, with Jay, so I can feed them. They are on minimum income, but he was expected to feed them both with no home 9-3pm and no accessible way to heat food or store it and of course the beer took priority.

I was happy to help. I got to see my son without a social worker and spend time together as a family. I'd send them back with food tubbed up and we hunted down a cool box. It's the best we could do.

West was now faced with the task of finding a house that takes housing benefit. He goes to every estate agent in town, the council and homeless shelter. No one can help. West was unemployed, so unable to afford private rent.

No refuge is available for men who are victims of domestic violence, and that's what he'd been told to say when surrendering the old house.

Men: fathers, do not have equal rights. He was bullied into an impossible position, which would force him to hand over his child and lose him for good. If social services aim to keep families together, why did they seemingly assure he was left homeless? We both quickly began to see the vast inequality of available help for male victims. It's quite disgusting.

After a few weeks he gets the threat; *'you have one more week to find a secure home, or our funding will cease, and we'll take Jay into care.'* A week later we send Jay to stay with Sally but the LA show up to remove him and take him into foster care.

We found out some years later, she asked them to take him, refused to care for him or adopt him herself, because she was too busy with her art degree.

Instead of calling us and saying that she couldn't keep Jay, and we needed to take him and plead with the LA, or at least have 24 hours to find another family member to help, she just rang the social worker, without even telling us what she was planning.

Once Jay was in care with Freya, it was over for our family. Sally is the reason both our kids ended up in care and subsequently adopted. She was always evil and manipulative and outright cruel towards me, even encouraging me to end my life on one occasion when I was 16. She did this for no other reason than, she's evil. No wonder West became what he was.

West had come to stay at my flat. He was literally homeless, and I couldn't turn a blind eye to that. Naturally, living together meant spending time together and we began to work on our marriage.
Neither of us having much in the way of a stable family life ourselves growing up, we were desperate to do right by our kids by being a strong and loving family unit. That's all either of us ever wanted from life.

We arranged an appointment with the 'children's guardian,' to discuss the developments going forward. We wanted to remain open and not be hiding things, like we had done previously about the food meets.

We had been caught a few days before. Ursula drove past as I was handing West a cool box of food. However, they never bought this incident up and my guess is they hushed it up in the court papers because I was having to feed them because West and Jay were not being provided adequate resources by the LA.

Our contact had just ended and once the kids had been packed into the car to go back to the foster carer, we sat and waited.

She made her way into the room with a poisonous smile, a smile full of falsity.

She reminded me of a giant slug. She seemed heavy in her movements and slow, like she was not quite sure how to function in her human body.

She sat opposite us and placed her notepad on her lap looking at us with such intent I could practically feel her eyes boring into my head as if searching for all my weaknesses. She introduced herself as Edith, the impartial representative for my children while care proceedings were in place.

We explain how we understand the LA's concerns about our relationship and its volatile history. We went on to discuss our current situation and hopes. We also made it clear, the only reason West ended up living with me again is because the homeless situation and no help being available. She nods knowingly.

We also request that we want to be assessed as individuals AND as a couple. Either of us is happy to do whatever it takes to keep the kids healthy and happy, and we know that may mean us parenting separately.

She thanks us for our honesty and tells us we will indeed be assessed as requested. We leave with a little hope. We had no idea the plan for adoption was already in place.

Freya is placed in the same home as Jay. West and I notice Freya does not seem to be crying so much anymore which is great for everyone. She was clearly more content with her sibling present and away from the previous carer who always seemed to view babies as transactions, not children.

Although I didn't really notice it at the time, looking back at pictures, Jay was hugely emotionally troubled at this point, and it was physically visible.

In pictures of him at our home, when we were all together, he is expressive, shiny, and wide eyed and always smiling. He is full of life and joy, being exactly as a toddler should be. But all the contact pictures show a different child, a drained child.

His eyes are matte without a single twinkle and his under eyes droop into dark bags, he does not smile and when we take pictures, we must ask him to pose, and he always arches his mouth in compliance but it's not even remotely real. It never reaches his small sunken eyes. His voice is flat, he moves slowly, and sounds bored a lot. It was like he hit puberty and became a stereotypical teenager before he was even out of nappies.

Chapter Four

The weather is beautiful the day we go to the city for our psychological assessment. The sun sits on my skin. It doesn't burn at all, it's a perfect midsummer day, despite my nerves.

Me and West talk on the train about what we think we will be asked.

It transpired I was the only one who was sent to a psychiatrist too for assessment. Which is weird because West is also mentally ill. But they only seem to care about me.

We arrive and I'm the first in. It was gruelling. I had to backtrack through my entire childhood, talking abuses and being encouraged to dish the dirt on mummy and daddy.

Dr Fawkes was a soft-spoken man who came across as caring and understanding. To this day, I will never understand how the LA appointed psychologists can sit and listen to these horrendous abuses and then shit all over the 'patient,' for money.

Did you know these so-called medical professionals can earn thousands per assessment? They get paid to break apart innocent families for profit. I'm sure Dr Fawkes was no exception.

He popped some cubes on the table. The cubes were red and off white, slightly scuffed and used around the edges.

He asks me to complete the puzzle. Not my strong point but I sit on the floor, at his feet, like a child and proceed to pick up every cube.

I put them all on the table and began to make formations. Normally I'd figure this sort of thing out in my head before physically doing it but being observed made me feel I could not do that.

I began to perspire under the observational pressure because I was nowhere near completion. I let out a frustrated sigh and say I can't do it. He tells me to keep trying and not give up so quick. I try again and within 2 minutes I succeed. That little bit of encouragement was all I needed. I smiled; I was really happy I'd done it.

Later West is called in and I sit in the waiting room and read magazines. I'm also given a strange bunch of questionnaires to fill out, as West had been. I remember scrolling along these questions and thinking 'what's being on the front of a magazine got to do with mental health or parenting?' Apparently, it was a test to see if I'm a narcissist.

"Ok, but what if I had been on a magazine?" I asked Dr Fawkes that and he cocked his head and smiled. Asking why and how the process worked was not acceptable. I just had to comply and do my tests. I ask questions to understand and as usual I was being shut down and made to feel stupid.

We are both called in for our joint assessment and it goes by without any drama. We are frank about our issues and faults.

It is arranged that Dr Fawkes will come and assesses us at the contact centre with the kids, the most stressful and unnatural environment going, because the LA insisted.

On the day of assessment we had not just Ursula but a psychologist observing us. It was a lot of pressure.

Freya cries through the contact. It turned out it wasn't just with me, as the contact supervisors had been telling me. She was the same for West too.

West plays with Jay. I try to soothe and comfort Freya who is, within 20 minutes, beetroot red and I begin to cry and feel a little overwhelmed, as do many mums when their baby cries constantly and cannot be soothed. I ask West to take her for a bit and see if he can calm her and I take on the roll of engaging my son.

Unfortunately, Jay wants to play with his dad. They do have a good bond and they were having fun, so he ignores my attempts to distract him. He's 2. He doesn't understand fully that daddy is busy right now and he's totally immune to his sisters screams.

29

I sit on the floor beside the 3 of them; deflated and exhausted. Eventually Freya calms down but stays in West's arms while he chats to our son and attempts to play with one free hand.

I continue to sit there, knowing I'm not required by my son right now. My tears have stopped but, I am visibly devastated by how this has gone. Contact was not always like this, but this was our one shot. The reports that came back were damning for me. However, West's report neglected to mention his abusive role in our marriage and his drinking and drug use was not drawn attention to apart from Dr Fawkes saying he'll need ongoing support to manage that and how it was due to his terrible childhood. But me, wow he tore me to shreds and my childhood trauma was no excuse for my bad behaviour.

Dr Fawkes stated that during contact, when I handed the screaming Freya to her dad, it was me not coping and needing someone else to take care of my baby. He felt, if I'd been alone, I'd have just left my baby in danger.

I argued this with the fact health visitors had told me to put my baby somewhere safe like a crib while I take a breath at distressing times.

He then ripped me apart for not engaging my son; for not being able to convince a small child he had to play with me and not his dad. Like I should have had total control of him.

He stressed that someone with my childhood could not parent, he diagnosed me with Borderline Personality Disorder (BPD), and suggested I'd need at least 5 years of intense therapy to be able to parent effectively and that was 'out of the children's timescales.' This being the little gem that tipped the scales in the LA's favour. The LA believe a child should be placed for adoption before it's a year old. This is because the older a child gets the less adoptable it becomes. Hopeful adopters usually want a new born or small child they can mould and shape and doesn't come with conscious memories, trauma or conditioning. They don't want to adopt an older child in the system who genuinely needs a home, so they don't age out of foster care. This desire is selfish and not child orientated at all.

The average court case in a family court is around 6 months for a new-born. Most professionals will prescribe a lengthy period of classes or therapy, which are often inaccessible due to poverty and location. This of course convinces the court adoption is the briefest and least damaging outcome for the child and total separation from the birth family is always the preferred plan for the future.

This pile of papers proclaimed nothing about me was right. I was a defective design and a sure disappointment to everyone I knew. Broken beyond repair, possibly dangerous, manipulative, self-loathing, and world's worst mum. The label etched itself into my life for many years to come, further isolating me and constantly making me a proprietor of others judgment.

That's the hardest thing in the aftermath of any adoption, consensual, coerced, forced or otherwise, everyone has their own perceptions and points of view and unless you have been through it, you cannot comprehend the magnitude of the injustice and pain, so much so you can't bring yourself to believe it.

Adoption challenges our social ideals and reality. This is often a home for labels, accusations, assumptions, and fogged thinking. All is not what it seems beyond the scales of justice.

Dr Fawkes had even mentioned the incident with the cubes, saying it was a sure sign I give up to quick *(further demonstrated by asking West to calm Freya)* and that I'd get frustrated and give up on my kids if I could not control them and then subsequently abuse and manipulate them to keep them in line, way into adulthood. It seemed his crystal ball had a grubby view of me.

I've never trusted a mental health professional since this incident and have withheld a lot of abuse from my childhood from them, in case it was used against me later.

It took me until my thirties to realise the LA had also abused and manipulated me, into silence with threats, gagging orders and shame. I believe this is what ultimately led to the bottling up of my grief and pain and getting very unwell in 2016 with Functional Neurological Disorder.

The LA had what they wanted but they still executed torturous psychological acts on me to keep me quiet and feeling weak and like the monster they were painting me out to be. I spent those five years he suggested in therapy, some years later, mostly undoing the long-term damage THEY CAUSED.

The sun is glorious today and it floods the floor of the contact centre. Edith and Callum have arrived to chat with me and West. Callum takes Jay aside to play while we fill out some forms. I look up occasionally and smile at how happy Jay is today. He's giggling and it feels so long since I heard that.

A scraping of plastic followed by shrill tears is had. Jay has fallen off a plastic toy box that Callum allowed him to climb upon to see outside.

I immediately raise from my chair and Jay reaches up as I approach. I take him into my arms where he gently sobs a bit while I kiss his forehead which now has a bump forming on it. He's quite happy for me being the one to soothe him and I feel a little touched by this. I ask Callum what happened, and he splutters about accidents while Edith seethes away out the corner of my eye at his momentous mess up. The heavy red glow in his face tells me he knows what happens when I leave.

I point out that accidents can happen to anyone, not just parents but social workers too and the room falls silent as West smirks at me approvingly.

Birth mothers are scapegoats for the adoption industry's failings.

Chapter Five

The summer continued to be sticky and warm. Our time with our kids was limited to an hour a week and we wait, believing that is all there is to do.

Our hair strand drug tests were back. West was given all clear. But me, I had, seemingly, be clean of drugs, right up until AFTER I had Freya. But the opposite was true, and documented. I was using cannabis until I was admitted to the ward and not used since.

They did not use this against me, clearly knowing the hair strand had been tested upside down, a small but not dismissible professional failure. It was brushed away. (pun fully intended)

I tried to query the competence of their chosen professionals, seems as they could not even test hair correctly, because I am pretty sure a good lawyer would exploit that small detail to their advantage. Tell me I am wrong! But my lawyer said it was insignificant and unfortunate and would not be of interest to a family court judge.

Dr Fawkes's reports favour West highly, in comparison to me. West is delighted his IQ is higher than mine, despite it being made clear it is due to age difference. He tells joke after joke about how superior he is. I laugh along because quite frankly, I know that IQ test did not mean a great deal in the grand scheme.

I now realise this was possibly done deliberately to cause friction between us, because his report was vastly different and excused his drinking; just like Callum had done back at the start of all this. This all confirmed to West he was a victim and me his source of pain and this allowed him even more control of me, allowing him to remind me for years to come how I was an 'abuser.' This would become his favourite word during any confrontation about his behaviour. A slur he'd shout in the street to humiliate me and cement the idea that I was the cause of so much wrong in our lives.

My physical aggression against West was, of course, a huge focus during the proceedings. It was concluded this behaviour was a result of my father who had beaten me and my mother. Looking back, I now see this was reactive abuse. West would push me to the very edge, waiting for me to lash out, never happy until I had struck him, and he could start using my violence against me to elicit sympathy from professionals.

No matter how hard I tried to walk away from an argument, get some space or even take a walk to calm down, he'd get into my face, belittling me and triggering me with a web of words. I quickly realised the sooner I hit him the quicker the situation would resolve. That's not to say my actions were fair. We are responsible for our behaviour and my temper was something I was struggling to manage at that time in my life.

The reports stated I could not develop and show true love because my mum failed to meet my emotional needs. I took drugs because I am easily led. The list of unforgivable sins within me was as eternal as the iron fist they seemed to be battering me with. I am so glad I lied and said I'd never been sexually abused. I think they would have ripped me a part like manic hyenas with a warm carcass.

Whilst still coming to terms and understanding my previous diagnosis of Bipolar, I was now being diagnosed all over again. I had only received my previous diagnosis a few months before. Although Dr Fawkes was sceptical to make the BPD diagnosis solid as he felt I would 'grow out of it.' This being due to my young age and hormonal changes. Hormones being the reason the LA claim these assessments can't be done whilst pregnant; they cannot gauge your true mental state but post birth and in distress they can.

35

We met with my lawyer, Irene, who assured us, although the report seemed quite damning, it didn't mean much, and we need not worry. We trusted her advice and awaited our final court date.

During this time, Edith was speaking to family and offering them a last chance to adopt our kids for us, to keep them with their birth family. The cost being, not being allowed contact with me and West directly for the kid's safety. This would possibly include moving away and an unknown location of the LA's choice.

Mum had just lost her partner suddenly after a major operation. She was drugged with diazepam and completely unfunctional, not to mention Dr Fawkes had blamed her for some of my defective existence. In the end she said she 'didn't want to give up her daughter.' Which to this day, feels ironic to me, coming from someone who put me in care because the now dead boyfriend had insisted on it.

My grandparents played on their age, despite being very well at the time, and said they could not afford to provide for Jay. They were happy to foster him, because they will get paid, like they had with me for a brief time as a teen, but the court didn't want the result of long-term foster care. They wanted adoption secured because that's what makes the figures look impressive and saves money.

Our entire family had now played a huge role in the permanent separation of us from our children, effectively devastating and dividing us all, forever and even then, no one bothered to inform us that the LA were planning to adopt the kids out.

Before attending court, a meeting would be held to establish that an adoption was the only way forward. West and I travelled to put across our case, this being the only time we really had the chance as we were never invited to court. I'm not even sure if court cases were being had to check the process.

We arrived and the foster carer was sat in the waiting room. We did not speak but she looked down at the floor and had a kind of nauseated look about her, like she might vomit any moment. I figured perhaps meetings made her anxious.

In the meeting they all agreed adoption was the only option. We expressed why we felt otherwise and some woman we'd never met came up with retorts that invalidated everything we said. It was incredibly frustrating to be shot down again and again.

They then called in the foster carer. They asked her how Jay and not Freya, would behave on returning from contact. She said he'd always return distressed and often cried. The room gave a sympathetic sigh about our son's sadness and decided it was a sign that seeing us was incredibly damaging for him.

We pointed out that perhaps he was distressed because he was constantly being taken away from his loving parents and not understanding why. The woman laughed and told us that was ridiculous. I don't, to this day, think it is ridiculous at all.

They then asked the foster carer if she agreed Jay and Freya should be placed for permanent adoption. Still solemnly looking at the floor, she gave a barely audible yes. She was then told she could leave, and she left so fast she became a blur. It was obvious she had been coerced into this and her guilt could not be contained.

Chapter Six

We attended court on a cold but dry December morning. It was bitter standing out the front of the big brown doors, waiting to be let in. The only people out there were West, me, mum and Irene.

We began to think the other party had given us the wrong place but alas, they were already inside, with the judges, nice and warm with cups of hot coffee.

Evidence was presented to the 3 judges, all visibly over age sixty, hook nosed and with tight-lipped smiles that look faker than clown makeup.

I do not recall much of that day. The part I remember most distinctly, was how pictures of my new flat were passed around for the entire room to see. Bear in mind, I lived in a one bed council flat, still did not have carpet or proper furniture because I'd lost everything back at the old house and these people were all in high paid jobs and wearing very posh suits, compared to my oversized second hand one. I felt small but I was proud to show how far I had come in a short time, during the time I had been away from West. I was already becoming aware he was part of my problem and I had hoped to at least achieve custody of the kids myself if not as a couple and have a reason to ask him to leave as I didn't want to keep living together at this point. He had been relatively decent those past few months, but I instinctively knew when the court case was over, my respite from him would also end.

After a morning of court activities, we broke for lunch. The LA piled into the nearest small sandwich shop, filling it, and making it noisy and awkward so we had to go further afield and eat in. They were almost pack like, how they swarmed into places and lives, destroying everything in their path.

On returning from lunch, the judges had decided they had deliberated enough on all the evidence in that hour and had made a choice. The children would be placed for permanent adoption against our wishes. The final family contact would take place the following week and myself and West's final contact would be 16th December.

I made a point of telling the judges how cruel they were to do this right before Xmas. I now understand, the kids would already be placed with the new parents, they were letting these strangers have their first Xmas with my children, whilst still infants. A great Xmas gift for the adoptive parents. But letting us have our last goodbye, after the proclaimed holiday of joy and goodwill, that was not a possibility.

I flipped. I left swiftly, kicking any chair that got in my way. I walked out onto the small and rammed roundabout; I hurled an entire case of ice scrapers into a road. I was furious and I wanted to kill anyone who dared challenge me. No one did, as I stormed through the market square tearing flower heads off. My blood felt hot in my core and my jaw clenched in rage.

I was calm by the time I arrived at a friend's house. The tea was sweet and hot and much needed after the cold air I'd been gasping in through heavy sobs. Eventually mum and West found me, calmed and somewhat blank. The repression had begun.

The final family contact was nice. We did a mini Xmas and gave the kids their gifts. Lots of pictures were taken, including the only one we have of us all together, three generations. Ironically, everyone looks depleted and dead inside, even Jay. Even while opening his xmas presents, Jay still doesn't smile or seem happy at all.

Freya has stopped screaming constantly at this point, having discovered her thumb which she now viciously sucks on at every opportunity. She cried if we tried to pull it out. This child was constantly self-soothing and highly anxious.

I remember Jay arrived with a huge ink smudge on his face. No one had washed it off and we tried to with what we had available, but it was not going to budge without redding his skin and causing discomfort. It was not a big deal but knowing he would have had his last pictures with his family that day, you'd think the foster carer would have kept him away from ink.

The end came and everyone does great, except nan. She proceeds to toss her walking stick on the carpark floor, grabs Jay, squeezes him aggressively and begins to cry and screech and wave her arms at Ursula who is trying to pry Jay out of this distressed woman's arms.

We calm her and Jay is perfectly fine and unfazed or harmed by the outburst.

Ursula, absolutely outraged, shoves West out the way and insists she straps Jay in this time so she can get him back quicker and prevent him further distress.

Although I can't stand my grandmother, can you blame her for her actions?

Me and West's final contact was taking place in the most non child friendly contact centre of all, 10 minutes from my home.

My hair was a deep magenta pink. It has been straightened, because it was almost Xmas and so nan paid for my hair to be done. I tried to look nice for the last visit with my kids. The following day, I cut it all off up to my chin.

We arrived on time and for once, so did Ursula. We had two hours that day, an extra special treat for us. So, it was me, West, the kids, Ursula, and Chris who we had not seen since we were all still a family back in our home, all crammed into a 10X10ft room. It is like Chris was there to see what she helped start, come to an end. Eyes digging. Elbows touching. Invasive.

It was not a bad time. We had bought a small cake, like it was a celebration. We took the icing pooh bear off the top and put it in a small tub. I told Jay we would keep it until he was a big boy. He didn't really understand and realistically it made little sense to keep it but that's what I told him as he nodded happily with a mouth full of cake.

Ursula and Chris laughed. And yes, maybe it is somewhat humorous, but this was being said by a mother trying to explain to her two-year-old son, she won't be seeing him for 16 years but that's not what she wants, and she'll keep holding on. There was no reality where that was an acceptable time to laugh. I kept it right up until I moved 12 years later, and it got smooshed.

The end of session came, and we didn't say anything, we got an extra 10 minutes as a result. We then had to put our kids coats on and prepare them to leave. They literally wanted us to pack them up and send them away while they watched. It is bordering psychological torture at this point.

I cry as I dress Freya and West is sorting Jay. Jay knows something is very wrong at this point even though West has kept face and we are both trying to smile.

We hug, all four of us and I put Freya in her car seat. Within seconds Ursula has scooped Freya's car seat from my hands and Chris has Jay by the hand.

I become hysterical, possibly facing for the first time, my reality. I remember asking them how they can do it. How could they just do that to people and not even look sorry? They would not make eye contact with us or our now crying son. No words, no nothing.

Jay was gripping the doorframe. I remember my eyes kind of zooming in on his knuckles and seeing how white they were. He was holding that door frame for dear life. He knew what was happening and he did not want it either. I ran towards him and was taken down immediately to the dusty hard floor. A weight lay atop of me, I was unable to move myself from the neck down. I laid upon the floor, this unknown entity atop of me, my head up and screaming for my son and him screaming right back.

Jay was saying no. He was calling for his mummy and daddy. This child was distressed and worse still, aware of his fate but not in a way he could fully understand.

The confusion must have been horrific. To never consciously be able to remember why he feels the way he does has to have lasting effects on his subconscious mind. This sort of early memory is not going to dissipate.

Eventually, after what seemed an eternity, Chris forcibly removed his tiny fingers from the door while Ursula made a dash for the car with Freya.

I heard my little boy screaming for his mummy. All the way out into the car park. I just laid there and cried into a silent corridor. Detached from the weight inside me and upon me.

Chris came back in after the kids had been driven off. She had the audacity to ask us if we were ok, as I still lay in a heap on the floor, staring at the wall, my husband looking down at me with no idea what to do with me. She then told us we could leave. That was it. Nothing else. No support, no next steps, nothing.

Chapter Seven

Life passes by. Chaos continues to collide with our lives. We cope in the ways the psychologist insisted was appropriate for people like us. West went about his addictions and me, being a horribly malfunctional borderline, did her thing.

 West and I grew a part; grieving in different ways over the next 3 years and destroying one another whilst I became the monster, I felt destined to be. Fawkes had stuck a label on me, and I was wounded deeply by it.

 No one explained what this BPD meant for me and the mental health team, before refusing to see me again, said it was not a mental health issue but a personality flaw, hence why they could not help. So, Dr Google was my lifeline. Back then BPD was vastly misunderstood, and the internet gave me a grim picture.

 Dr Fawkes had done such a great job convincing me this was who I was, I began to shift. My purpose in life was to be all or nothing and then dead, a mere statistic. Convinced I was worthless I went about my life, with no care for anything, especially me.

 During the court proceedings my mother's partner passed away. I had not got along with him, having been a victim of his emotional and physical torture since age 9. But she was distraught, and my grief did not matter, it was not comparable and all my time in the following months of losing my kids were dedicated to watching over and mothering her.

 I didn't even get to live in my own house and sleep in the same bed with my husband because I had to stay with mum. Then 6 months later she met her now husband and within the year they were married. So, I went from playing nurse and watchguard to wedding planner and never got my chance to grieve, something she screamed in my face one day while I was crying, like it had been my choice not to grieve my loss in the moment. I don't recall her once ever asking how I was feeling about missing my kids. She was wholly consumed by her needs until she had a new partner to care for her.

I did not suffer all the time. I had fun. I resumed alcohol and cannabis and I did a lot of partying. I cannot say I was ever bored in that time. I was happier when not with West, but he just would not leave me be.

I kept trying to start my new life, but he kept attempting suicide and then getting the hospital to call me, as I was still down as next of kin, and we were married. Even after he got his own home the saga continued for many years. He destroyed any relationship I attempted to have, put a wedge between me and any new friends I made and even continued to introduce me as 'my wife' I was never me; I was his property. To this day, those 2 tiny words feel like nails on a chalkboard to me.

He would hoover me back in every time with guilt. Frequently stating only we could understand one another because nobody else had been through our loss and we needed one another. He had me convinced I needed him as much as he demanded me. This manipulation went on for another 14 years.

At one point West moved to The City with his mother. I was finally free because he wanted to be free. His mum then helped him concoct a story that he attacked a paramedic and was now in prison. So, when I attempted to divorce him, my solicitor was sent on a wild goose chase trying to hunt down a prisoner who did not exist. I had also been encouraged to use this incarceration as a means for my divorce. So of course, in the end, it looked like I was lying, and I felt stupid and gave up trying to get the divorce. Somehow, he had managed to keep me, again.

Summer 2008, I unexpectedly conceived my third child, Meadow. An unpleasant surprise I'm afraid to say. This was not what I wanted at all.

After months of eating no more than 1000 calories a day, I was finally almost at my desired weight. I was not happy about getting fat again. I was wholly consumed by an eating disorder at this point, desperate to have some control of one thing in my life. I knew that I'd have to eat proper food to sustain the child and lose that small piece of control I did have.

I had been surviving off chocolate, veggie burgers, sugary tea, and occasional family meals to keep mum quiet. I was fully aware I was damaging myself. I just did not care.

Finding out I was pregnant, immediately changed everything. I was finally unable to ignore all the issues around me.

Meadow's dad was young; no older than I was when I was stuck at home with a baby. In all truth, I didn't want that for him or for the child who would be raised by him. Even I had not behaving like an adult.

The rumour mill began to do its thing. Within a week of finding out, I knew I had to get out of that circle and away from his family, fast, even though I was booked to have an abortion at 9 weeks. I was in a bad place, and I could not stay there.

I had been trying to break it off anyway, but I had once again found myself in a toxic situation where I'd be threatened and manipulated if I tried to break free. Eventually the police did have to step in, and he was charged with harassment. The devastation I'd bought upon my life in grief suddenly slapped me in the face. Over night I went from wild child metal head to mum.

It was just under 3 years since I lost Jay and Freya and I truly didn't think I could do it again. My mother also took the time to remind me, *'it's not fair on the rest of the family.'* By this time, she had remarried, and I had a great stepdad and step grandparents. But they never suffered the previous loss. She was making it about her needs as usual and never once mentioned how another loss may impact ME. She made it clear I did not have their support and I was not to tell nanny and I would have a quiet abortion at the day clinic. I never questioned it and accepted the entire family would be against me. But it turned out to be far from true.

She took me for the confirmation scan and insisted I was not allowed to look at the screen, luckily the sonographer realised it was my baby and not my mums and proceeded to show me and to sooth me it was the size of a small fingernail and then mum chimed in that it was not a baby at all. I confirmed, with guilty tears in my eyes, I wanted to kill the bean on the tv.

Mum and Rob were on holiday the week the abortion was booked. I was staying at mum's house to cat sit and I rose that morning, numb. I sat on the sofa to have a cuppa and never got up again. I sat there until bang on 12, after my abortion should have been done.

Mum realised I was not answering texts and calls before my appointment and knew I had not gone. When I finally answered a call, she was furious. I had ruined her holiday and her life. I was keeping this burden.

At 9 weeks, I informed social services of my pregnancy. I was not going to wait for the midwife to do it, I had nothing to hide, felt confident I'd done well and would manage this situation fine without West, or any other man. I called, asked to speak to anyone on the previous case but was told I could not. So, I just left a message for anyone who it concerned.

Adoption completes families but often at the expense of another family's misery

Chapter eight

Most prebirth assessments, should start around 16 weeks into the pregnancy to give an extended view of the mother's capability to parent her child. So, I was well ahead of the clock. But that time came and went, and nobody had called or mentioned my previous kids. The midwives had no concerns and had not heard anything either. I was starting to get a little excited thinking this may not end in disaster.

Months rolled by. I was in my third trimester when the phone finally rang with the call I'd dreaded. I was way past the cut-off date for that abortion now. I had to go ahead with this pregnancy.

A brand spanking new male social worker was on my case. Keen and fresh out the illusion social worker school clearly creates, he firstly apologised for '*making another pregnant woman cry.*' That rang alarm bells straight away. Clearly, I was not the first mum to get the call that day.

Paul told me they'd be informed RECENTLY of my pregnancy, and he needed to have several meetings with me for this assessment. He went on to explain he didn't know about the previous case and didn't need to because the idea was we start again and asses who I am now. He made is sound very fair and positive and I suddenly felt a lot less worried. Everything he said ended up being a lie.

I disliked him instantly if I am honest. This weedy sunken faced man was cocky and sarcastic. He tested my patience from the start. He told me I could not voice record the sessions to provide evidence should the case go to court. He asked a lot of questions about West, who I had not been with in quite some time. He then asked what I thought happened with my other kids and if I agreed with the adoption. He asked the most audacious questions, largely about things he said would not matter in this assessment.

Nothing I said was right. I did not know the baby's gender at this point so when I referred to the child as *'it"* I was written up for that because apparently it meant I was emotionally detached from the child. Even if I did have some attachment issues, could you wonder at it? I was attempting to prepare for a baby I was not wholly, if at all convinced, I was going to be allowed to keep.

He asked to see what I had bought the baby. I had a chest of draws in my room with the baby stuff I'd so far collected. I pulled out some basic items to demonstrate I had clothing, bedding and age-appropriate toys but I had apparently not opened every box or draw and given an enthusiastic, enough demo. I tried to explain, I assumed as a man he did not really want to hear me discuss my child's entire wardrobe collection. But he insisted I was not *'engaged'* with my pregnancy. He was nit-picking at the tiniest details because there were no actual issues to be found. It was quite pathetic.

One time he arrived, shamed me for eating so much chocolate (a few wrappers were on my coffee table) then commented I'd get too fat.

Another time he left and pointed to a nearby Slipknot poster and told me that had to come down off the wall before he saw me again. Genuinely confused I asked why. He told me it was not appropriate for the baby and would cause *'it'* distress. My newborn baby would be damaged beyond repair by this A4 sized poster that would likely be gone by the time the child had any realisation of its surroundings anyway. Amused, I agreed to remove it.

When the report was written he mentioned that poster. He said it depicted bondage and sexual aggression and I had refused to remove it *(rather than just questioning it)* and had argued with him about it.

That simply was not true but because I had not been allowed to record or document the session, I had no proof that what had been said, was said. The only gospel evidence in me and my unborn child's case, was anything he had provided. My musical taste was deemed dangerous and now so was I.

Around this time, I had a 4D scan and was able to find out I was certainly having a baby girl. It was a wonderful experience in which mum and Rob accompanied me.

Afterwards we went to Tesco and there I finally bough my first girls' clothing item. An adorable and tiny red jumper with little white flowers all over it. I still have it to this day, but I never did get to see Meadow wear it.

Whilst all this was going on, we as a family, were also putting plans in place for the court. The LA did not tell us about *'family group conference meetings* (FGC).'Where the idea is, family members meet, with a social worker present, to help establish a plan of action to keep the child safe and with the family. The LA were astonished how we had come across this and when we refused to say and played them at their own game, they reluctantly agreed to attend the first meeting only. They outright refused to comply to the usual proceedings because even then, their only goal was adoption.

So, the family gathered at the contact centre, the place where so many of my last days with my kids were spent. Our 'supervisors' who were known on a personal level by a family member, informed us of our rights and let us know they managed to get the funding for the food. Another thing the social worker did not want to provide.

Paul arrived late with a higher up colleague. She quite literally looked like Ms Trunchbull and had an attitude to match. Her name was Karen.

They explained they did not support this approach. I asked why and she refused to elaborate. This was before my assessment was even over.

They gave us a single piece of paper, not the full files and concerns that we requested so we could help the court and LA feel more at ease that we were taking their concerns seriously. They then said they would not be staying or coming again, handed me a section 21 and urged me to sign it. Our supervisors were livid. A quick shouting match ensued where Karen was reminded you never bring a section 21 to an FGC meeting and that it was the most unethical thing she could have done. We heard them grilling her that the whole point was to prevent that and the fact she came just to do that was sickening behaviour and unprofessional.

We finally had people linked to the LA who saw the lack of empathy and ethics I was being subjected too. We all sat in the next room silently giggling as she attempted to justify it just to be shouted down.

A section 21 is the paperwork that a parent signs to allow the LA to place a child for adoption. It was only now, with this explanation from someone not making money from my child's adoption, that I realised what I had signed in the psych ward that time, was in fact this form.

On this occasion they had come to ask me, in front of my entire family, and professionals from another department, to give up my baby willingly because I had no chance. They were trying to intimidate me. I ripped it up in front of them and put it in the trash can beside me and smiled. It remains to this day, one of the proudest moments of my life. I was not what they thought. I was not going to lay down and play dead, I was going to fight this, and I would not be stopped.

We did our best with limited resources to tackle all concerns. Even my bio dad attended these meetings
to help. The only people who did not were my nan and grandad, who did not like my step grandparents. As always, my grandmother's pettiness would not allow her to help me.

With the support of the supervisors and around four sessions of four-hour meetings we came up with a solid plan to make sure I was supported 24/7 with the child until the authorities were satisfied. This would involve me giving up everything, including my home and freedom, to be watched by family 24 hours a day, for the foreseeable future. We were willing to do so much to show how much we as a family wanted this child.

They didn't even look at the proposed plan before they called the final meeting to announce they were seeking a care order, nor did they have it in the paperwork to submit to the court and my solicitor said it was no use and she would not be handing it in either.

We were furious, including the professionals who had never seen their work and efforts dismissed quite so quickly. One of them made sure our plan did make it to a judge eventually. At great personal risk. None of it was worth it in the end. When it was briefly raised in court, it was shot down with how my family would not be able to recognise if I was abusing Meadow. This royally offended nanny who has spent her entire adult life running Scouts, undergone child protection training, filed reports and even won awards for her services to children.

The day of judgment came. Nanny took a now 37 weeks pregnant me to the dank building they called an office. We were all sat around the large mahogany table, hard chairs beneath us, the smell of musty mothballs swirling in my nostrils; heavy and suffocating, waiting for the late members of their party. It was me and nanny against Paul, 2 lawyers, the manager; Maureen, Karen, a policeman, midwife, and some random faces I had never seen before. This was my first time meeting the manager, the head honcho of the hyenas, who had overseen my previous kid's case.

To be sat around this large table with all these strangers deciding the fate of the unborn child inside me was vile. Their cold and callous attitude made me feel like shrinking, sucking my stomach in to keep their greedy claws off my child.

The midwife arrived very much in support of me and my case to keep my child and during this meeting verbalised her and her colleagues had no concerns going forward and I had shown no signs of any issues and that I had been very compliant, had all my tests and was stable. They then questioned had she seen the PAST paperwork, you know, the stuff Paul had told me wasn't going to be important. She had not so they gave her a very brief rundown of the outcome only and asked her again if she had concerns. She confirmed currently she did not and then with reluctance and avoiding eye contact with me, she agreed the past was worrying and she agreed the child should go into care. Turns out they needed a unanimous decision to go ahead.

The clean slate was a myth and only the past mattered. Who I was in that moment stood for nothing. With that, the manager slammed her folder shut, the lawyer nodded in agreement and closed his files, and everyone began to leave. Nanny was desperately trying to get heard. They made the choice and just cut us off and left us standing in a large silent room. It was comparable to the aftermath of the final contact I had had with my children just a few years before. We had just been stonewalled.

Not everything that falls to the ground is destined for death, birth is the by-product of knowing when to let go

Chapter Nine

I spent the remaining 3 weeks of my pregnancy, trying to stay positive. Then at midnight, bang on her due date, I awoke to a sharp pain in my belly, and I knew instantly it was time. I called mum and begun to prepare sandwiches while I waited for her to arrive.

I got in the car. Daddy Rob realised my waters had not yet broken and begun to drive in haste to make sure I did not eject the contents of my now violently contracting womb into his car.

Birth was a better experience this time. I was not a prisoner or treated like one. There was no police presence that I know of and by 4 am, the whole process was over.

I had intended another water birth, but I got the urge to push so the midwife was reluctant to move me to the room next door in case standing caused me to pop my sprog in the corridor. It still ended up being another 2 hours.

When my waters did break, they were very brown and yellow and I knew the baby had loosened its bowels, likely in distress. Distress it was likely picking up of a mother that did not want to birth it because she knew it meant loss for her.

The midwife was not worried and dismissed my mums concerns and I carried on labouring. Eventually she did notice the meconium, and called a paediatrician to check Meadow over, after she emerged.

It was the worst 5 minutes of my life, seeing my baby wrapped and laid out on a table across the room, unable to hold her while I awaited yet another medical professional's judgment and assumptions that I was the issue. He quickly confirmed she was fine and handed her to me. We were both safe and well.

By 8 am I was wheeled, with my baby, to the maternity ward, where I would stay for 7 days, awaiting a court date, because I still had not signed the section 21. Without that, they couldn't just take her, I could make them fight for once. The only condition was, I couldn't leave the hospital. I was told, despite her being my child entirely, if I left, it would be classed as kidnap, and I'd be arrested, and an emergency care order would be made. Basically, I had to comply or lose her quicker. It made no sense but the fret of being sent to prison for kidnapping your own offspring is quite frightening.

I remember nanny asking me how I felt, after 4 days. I told her it felt like I was waiting on death row. There was little to no hope, I felt like I was being sentenced to death except at the end of this stay, I'd live to tell the tale of my agony.

My biological father cried when he left and that's saying something. Nan and grandad visited once, showing little to no emotion and I did not blame them. Mum and West visited almost every day. Between these visits' I'd sit and stare at my sleeping baby, breastfeed and hold her. There was nothing to do but sit and wait in our cubicle.

Court was meant to be on the third day, but the LA cancelled last minute. It was done to test and torture me. There was zero need to keep me there that long. They wanted me to get distressed and go home so they could take Meadow and get dirt on me to do it.

The CAFCASS guardian was assigned, and it was Edith. So much for fresh starts and not focusing on the past. She came to visit, and we were given a private room to chat in. I sat in the chair with Meadow asleep in her cot. Edith leered over, smiling like a loon, eyes wide as she hungrily looked at my baby. It was diabolical to see literal pound signs in her eyes. My gut clenched as she reached to touch, and I put my hand out and rubbed Meadow's head and she retracted her arm as though I had bitten her and sat herself on the bed.

We both gave one another fake smiles, pretending all was well and cooperative.

She explained the local authorities plan, to seek a care order whilst I undergo assessments to make sure I am suitable to parent my child. She acknowledges I do not consent, and I am against this. She smiles the entire time she talks. It is almost like someone paints her face on each day, making her joy unmovable, despite the misery around her.

So, for 7 days and nights, I sit, perfectly healthy and taking up space in an NHS bed, trying to explain to other mums why me and my baby were there. I am met with mixed reviews. Naturally, some turn away from me, assuming this means I am some kind of child abuser and others sympathise and seem astounded because I am *'such a good mummy.'*

The midwives who have come to know me or about my case, frequently stopped by to confirm they also do not agree with this. They would happily hire a bus to get every midwife to the court and tell them this, but they never actually do. Maybe if professionals cared more about the community they serve than their reputation and wage, they would make a difference. But I was fast realising people were all talk when it mattered.

The day of doom rolls around. I dress as best I can and reluctantly leave my baby with the staff, who take her to the special baby unit.

The magistrate court is bustling with small-time criminals. We are ushered up to the top floor, where the crown court resides. West was there. My lawyer, Rashford, a gormless looking man who constantly sounded bored, explains the LA had decided because he visited me in the hospital, he must be the baby's dad. He was given 48 hours to get ready for court. So, with no solicitor, he came to court, to defend us himself and prove he is not the father. It was a nerve-wracking position to be put in.

It was a long day. For months after, other lawyers would approach me in court and ask about my case.

We ended up at the court that day from 9 am until 11 pm. The judges took 5 hours to deliberate and come to their conclusion. This was unheard of in a family court. This told me what I needed to know; they were struggling to win this one, but I knew that also meant they would up their game to assure their win. I was right.

They started by questioning Paul. He was quite submissive against Karen, who had clearly primed him for this event. He later tried to pipe up during her questioning, to correct her on what he had said. It was in my defence. Every single one of them turned in their chairs and shushed him aggressively. Even I winced. The judges pretend not to notice this outright lie that was being hushed up.

Karen, who has never actually spoke to me outside of asking me to sign the section 21, had a lot to say during her time on the stand, until West gets his time to question her.

She point blank refuses to answer him. Showing an utter disrespect to him, despite the fact he's allowed to defend himself, she refuses to treat it as such and outright ignores him. He asks her questions over and over, while her colleagues snicker together about it. They were trying to enrage him, but it does not work, and I am so proud of him in that moment.

Despite this, the judges do absolutely nothing. In a criminal court, this would not have been acceptable. She refuses to acknowledge any positive changes I made, not even the fact I have given up smoking for my baby's health. She will not budge.

I sit there absolutely gobsmacked at her childish behaviour, skin crawling at these so-called professionals openly laughing like a pack of excitable hyenas, at the frustration it was causing. It was grotesque.

She stubbornly holds onto her pettiness until the questioning is passed over to her own solicitor, where she suddenly found her voice again, loud, and clear.

The outright corruption and refusal to work with the family was blatantly obvious and the judges did absolutely nothing. Now, tell me, in any criminal court, would any of the above have been overlooked or would it find its way to the jurors' minds and cause them to think there was something to hide? Bear in mind, family courts do not have a jury, only a judge or judges, connected to the local authority.

Time passes. We even skip lunch to get this done. So, by afternoon I am hungry, missing my baby and worst of all, absolutely soaked through with breast milk. My top is soaked, and I had to take the stand with milk pooling upon my chest. I sat hunched and embarrassed and definitely did not feel confident in myself and what I was about to do.

As I stood and everyone noticed they all put their heads down as if they wanted to spare me my shame. Nobody suggested we stop for a break so I could go change or at least shove a copious amount of tissue into my soggy bra.

Their ability to switch off their humanity and common decency haunts me to this day. I find it hard to believe some of them were even human at all.

The LA solicitor did his best to trip me by repeating the same questions with different words and being pedantic as possible. I reply with the same truthful answers and keep my cool. The truth is, they have nothing here, not a leg to stand on. The judges ask me questions and seem genuinely interested and impressed with all I have managed to achieve in three years and it's then I realise, this guy, was the judge on my previous kids final hearing. Surely if anyone can see a change here, it's him.

I sit back down after my time on the stand. I am still wet and very cold in the April snap. TheLA manager decided then was a perfect time to open a window as wide as possible. I'm shivering within thirty seconds and my mum politely points this out, but she just smiles sadistically and does not close it. We cannot react. I must sit there and let them nit-pick in the attempt to cause me to explode. They fail.

Around 6 pm we are finally done giving evidence and can go eat and change. We don't get given more than an hour, because that's what's normal, so mum and Rob dash for dry clothes and breast pads and food asap. I stand in the basement toilet, in a top that's now so wet it drips milk onto the grey stony floor. The band of my trousers is now wet and even the back of my top has saturated, and I reek of sour milk.

59

Edith lumbers into the bathroom and completely overlooks me; it's like I am invisible.

We scoff down our much-needed food believing we have just minutes. Five hours passed before we were called back into the court for the judgement.

During the extensive wait, we sat and chatted. Whilst doing so, we saw Edith entering the judge's chambers. We all know that members of the public, defence, jury or otherwise, are not to enter judge's chambers, especially during a trial. But there she was, bold as brass, walking in and sitting herself down like an old friend. We raise this issue with Rashford who informs me that yes, it's not allowed but she's a *'powerful woman.'* Again, this outright defilement of due respect and law, was being flounced in our faces. She was in there, making sure she got what she needed because she knew, the fact those judges were not out within the hour meant I was winning. We all knew that. I'd loved to have been a fly on the wall in that room.

Chapter Ten

We are called back into the court room just before 11 PM and although, deep down, I already know what's coming, I keep a brave face and a hopeful heart.

The judges make it clear, especially to Edith, that they have 6 weeks to conduct their assessments with the psychologist and that their care order is for 6 weeks only. I'm furious my baby is going into care, but I know I can prove myself in these assessments and it's just 6 weeks.

The LA party literally breathe a sigh of relief. They got what they came for.

We all pile out of the room. I am in tears, unable to even breathe at this point and Karen is trying to start a conversation with me. Rashford recommends she leaves and now is not the time to try and get sensible conversation out of a distressed mother. This is the only time he does anything to actually help me.

My face is now as wet as the rest of me. I am tired and shutting down. I chose to return home and sleep and bathe, leaving the baby at the hospital. For some reason, distancing myself seemed like a good idea at the time.

At around 4 am the next day, I wake, dress and plan to visit Meadow then it's off to the multistorey car park to commit suicide. I do not want to live without her.

I walk up to the hospital early and go to SCBU. They are pleased to see me and let me in no issue to be with my baby. I am given privacy to just hold my baby and cry knowing this is my last private moment with her. It's around 7 am at this point. Social workers typically start their day around 9 am so I had a while or so I thought.

Not long after I arrive, Karen and a new social worker assigned to my case, Lacey, arrive full of smiles to collect their *new foster baby.* If I had not shown up when I did, I'd have come back to an empty crib. They were absolutely determined to remove her asap. I asked what happened to Paul and was told he was no longer on the case. Speaking up to defend his own words in court had clearly had consequences in his career.

We were transported to a private room. The new girl introduced herself while Karen towers over the crib gasping at how perfect my baby is. My stomach curdles. She's looking at my tiny baby like desirable meat. Her eyes are wide and bright, and I can see almost every tooth in her head. She is deliriously happy to be taking this baby from me. She then gruffly begins to put Meadow's stuff into a bag and tells me I can leave. Lacey literally cringed at her colleague's brusque attitude and gave me a sympathetic smile. I said goodbye, calmly, and left. No one knew my intention after this.

My mum and West were waiting for me. They had rung and asked if I was there, and the staff explained what was happening. They were waiting for me because they knew me well enough to know what I would plan next.

I return home and have a brief meltdown. I begin to throw all the baby things out the front door, as my mum and West attempted to catch it all and throw it back in. We must have looked quite absurd to anyone watching, like a humorous attempt at training for rugby but this moment was far from funny. I am utterly void of any hope in that moment and my pain is raging, burning my blood into a bubbling bitter brew. Every fibre of my being was tainted by this injustice at what was happening to me and my baby girl.

Six weeks went by. I travelled by train 3 times a week to see Meadow. I was only given this amount of time because the court insisted, I should be allowed to continue to breastfeed, seems as Meadow had settled into it so well during our 7 days in hospital. But my breasts quickly began to become painfully full, and the midwives told me to stop, or I'd likely end up with blocked ducts and infections. So, I took their advice. Naturally I was judged harshly for this and reminded so much contact had only been granted because of the breastfeeding. They wanted me to ignore the midwife's advice and continue. Within a week, I was in so much pain, I had to stop. I couldn't even feed Meadow anymore I was so swollen and full.

I didn't have any ongoing post birth care after I went home because I did not have a baby. No one ever come to check my muscles had healed or that I was not experiencing post birth issues. I was once again having my health neglected because the LA had my child.

Court soon rolled back around. The same 3 judges would be there, and a different solicitor was sent out for me. I quickly began to realise there was no consistency on my side. It was a new face all the time.

Despite being told previously, that the psychological assessments that the LA insisted be done, must be done so within this 6 week period, nothing had been done, not even a referral. The judges were furious.

It was visible on the man's face he had been outright defied, and he was not happy. He reluctantly gave them another 6 weeks to get it sorted. We never saw that trio of judges again.

Months went by. I continued contact 3 times a week, never failing to turn up or arrive on time. I did all the activities they asked me to do including bath the baby and take her to be weighed or out on my daily errands.

Eventually contact took place at my home. I had not been given this previously and I started to take it as a good sign that reunification was their goal. I now wonder if it was just a desperate attempt to find fault and the more time I had, the more chance they had to fail me on this warped assignment.

The contact supervisors were a mixed bunch. All of them, including the foster carer Meadow was staying with, said I was a good mummy and how well I was doing. I now know they were grooming me with false hope and trust, attempting to make me comfy around them.

One woman was telling me how Meadow had been the main subject in the office recently. She proudly told me how pretty everyone thought Meadow was, and that Lacey hoped if she had a baby one day, it would be as pretty as Meadow. Alarm bells were ringing in my ears. Not only did these people have a picture of my child to share in their office but a pretty baby meant highly adoptable. I knew then my chances were wholly gone but I continued to fight anyway.

The psychologist assessment was finally booked, and the LA now want to consider sending me away to a mother and baby unit for in-depth assessment.

My assessment with Dr Fawkes was considerably shorter this time. I did not have to repeat the cubes, questionnaires or be retraumatized by talking about my abuse. He made it clear he felt I had done 'extremely well,' to have come as far as I had in those 3 years, and I had exceeded his expectations.

The LA had asked him to investigate my love of heavy metal music and how this would impact my child if I should raise her. They were clutching at straws with this one. Dr Fawkes explained in his assessment that people who had suffered the traumatic life I had (he was acknowledging my pain this time around) often turned to music and artists such as these bands because they are relatable and give way to creative expression and it in no way said anything about me as a person or proved I was a risk to my child. It was clear from the way he apologised for even having to ask, that he felt this was a damn circus.

He said he would not be advising they sent me, alone, to the mother and baby unit 2 hours away from my friends and family, as he felt that would be 'setting me up to fail.' He would be strongly suggesting they allow me to stay with my support system. It was all very positive, and I had faith his testimony would benefit me and my darling girl.

Again, court soon fell upon us. But the LA were not happy with Dr Fawke's assessment and felt a second opinion was needed. The new judge, no doubt a pal of Edith, was more than happy to allow it. The worst part, the new doctor I'd be seeing was a friend of Karen and she had insisted the LA send me to her, despite having never been involved in adoption assessments.

It seemed they didn't like the fact Dr Fawkes had been pro mum this time, so they continued to seek the answers they needed to secure the adoption.

I'll never forget that assessment. Dr Dru was, for want of a better word, cool. She greeted me in a biker style jacket and boots, her blond hair wild and wavy like mine. I, being very much into my rock and metal, thought she was fabulous for a woman her age. She certainly broke the mould when it came to what medical professionals look like. Dr Dru had a whole different vibe to any other professional I'd met. I couldn't for the life of me work out how she had ever made friends with someone as stoic and plain as Karen. She had invited me to her big fancy home for my assessment and on arrival I was walked through a beautiful large house, to a spacious conservatory looking out over a stunning flower garden. I was mesmerized. It was the type of home you find on a vision board.

We talked for several hours. It was hard work, some tears were shed, especially talking about my future with Meadow. At this point my inner knowing already knew she'd be gone soon and when asked *'what do you see in your future without Meadow?'* I replied *'nothing, it's totally black.'*

I don't know if she really understood what I was conveying but I was discreetly (due to nanny's presence) trying to tell her I wasn't planning to live at all without my daughter.

It was another positive assessment for me. She was also against sending me away to the unit. Basically, I had passed both tests with flying colours and the family were all thrilled. Maybe Meadow would come home after all.

This woman never speaks to me at the bus stop. But today she is offering her condolences about the loss of my child. I quickly realise she has me confused with the other Annie who lives on our street. She's seen me pregnant and now I'm not and she thinks it's me who had to lower that tiny white box into the ground.
What do I do? I can't let her believe my baby died but if I tell her the truth, will she judge me? I politely correct her and explain she's thinking of another lady. She asks where mine is as she never sees me with it. I explain the basics of what happened in court and the plan going forward. There is no more sympathy for my loss, even if it does end up being forever. I'm a birth mother, my baby breathes, I should just be happy with that.
I know the whole estate will know soon enough. The next day, no one says hello to me at the bus stop.

Neither society nor the adopter, who holds the child in her arms, wants to confront the agony of the mother whose arms that same child was taken – Margaret Lawrence

Chapter Eleven

Court could not come quicker for me. However, both assessments were all but dismissed and the court gave permission to send me and Meadow away to the unit for 12 weeks of full-on 24-hour observation, like a criminal. Although it is worth noting, even prisons don't watch you 24/7.

It seemed absurd to me, that the 9 hours a week contact I'd been doing, with various everyday activities, had not been enough time for them to observe me in action as a mother. I had demonstrated bathing, nappy changing, prepping and feeding milk and solids, play time, attending appointments and putting my child to bed.

We would end up attending court roughly every 6 weeks for 10 months. Each time, little progress having been made on their part and them never being satisfied.

We asked when family members would be assessed to be carers for Meadow. With a roll of the eyes, Edith agreed to assess my step grandparents only.

On the day, she could not find the correct house. Nanny, luckily, saw her wandering about outside and preceded to chase after her. By the time she got outside, Edith was hot footing it to her car. Nanny called her name; it would have been impossible not to hear her on a quiet cul-de-sac. She got back in her car and drove right past my nan on the way out. No alternative assessment date was offered.

A few weeks before the residency began, Lacey and one of the contact girls took me there for a meeting. During that interview, I was asked if I am breast feeding and I said no. Lacey butted in that I had been, but I quit. In that moment I saw red, and she knew it. Quit was not the word.

I never raised my voice, but I gritted my teeth and glared at her muttering dangerously, *'and who's fault was that?'* There was so much venom in that moment I could see I had scared her, and I had no remorse. How dare she try to shame me in front of these people for a choice they had taken from me and my baby. Needless to say, the car trip back was uncomfortable and I'm glad because that meant she got two hours of what my life had been like all those months.

I could tell Lacey was just starting in her career and very naive to what was expected of her and what actually happens in these cases. She had not yet developed the ability to shut off her emotions, lie convincingly or hide her awkwardness at the obvious cruelty towards me that she sometimes witnessed. I believe I was her first case and by the end of it, I pitied this girl. I now have remorse about how I spoke to her that day. I acted off pure emotion because I felt attacked.

The day of the residency quickly came. Nanny drove me there, ahead of Meadow, so I had time to unpack and get everything in place. We had been there all of 10 minutes when Lacey arrived with Meadow several hours early. Deliberately of course, to see how I'd cope unboxing and caring for a child, alone.

Nanny was told to leave; she was not allowed to stay and help, and I'd not be allowed visitors for the first month while we settled in. That was news to us. Naturally I panicked. No family for a month. They knew exactly what they were doing to me. I truly was being set up to fail. Not once at the meeting had that been raised.

I was terrified and alone, in a strange place, hours away from home, with no money for phone credit, just me and a baby under constant judgment. But I pulled up my socks and did the best I could.

I had to give up smoking, because I was not allowed out for a cigarette with the baby but also not allowed to leave her alone, unless she was asleep in her cot and then I was allowed 5 minutes. They made my time there as hard as possible.

All the other parents there were allowed to have baby monitors or bring their baby outside into the enclosed garden but not me. I was being treated totally differently to the others. Even the other mums were confused.

Most of these people were young women, who blew smoke on their babies, swore loudly and gossiped and had no sense of being a grown up about them. Nor were they constantly followed about. But

I noticed something about 2 of the.... less charming mums, their babies had physical defects. Meaning, not highly adoptable.

One of these women would eventually be allowed to take her child home, despite her previous child being removed due to actual neglect less than 2 years before. She sat there and told me that as though it were nothing. I felt sick as a pig knowing that the only reason this irresponsible girl was going home with her kid was because it was not deemed adoptable.

When I arrived at the unit, I was given a parenting manual, you know, the one we get told doesn't exist. Well, there is a government correct way to raise a child but only those of us who find ourselves at the mercy of the LA get to see it.

There was a strict protocol on how I had to do everything from making a bottle, changing a nappy, to how to interact with my baby. I had to read it all within 24 hours because if I did not do these things in the correct way, it would be considered bad parenting and I'd have this used against me.

In just a day, I had to care for my baby, unpack and read an entire book. It was all quite ludicrous.

I think I lasted 3 weeks in all. I very quickly became depressed and tearful and began cutting my legs again, discreetly, in the bathtub. They made me see a local GP who gave me medication, that my actual GP would never have given because they knew it caused manic episodes. I knew I could not take them.

My mental health rapidly declined, as predicted by both Doctors. I begged the LA to let West, to whom I was still married, come stay with me so they can assess us as a family. I was that desperate to stay and make it work but I was struggling to do so alone, and he was the only 'family' with no job. It was a act of sheer of hopelessness.

They said no of course, they already had what they wanted, me failing as a mother. But then, they were told sending me here, with zero support or meaningful and safe connections, would be the very thing that caused me to fail. They used both doctor's main concerns to achieve their greedy means, no matter what it did to me and Meadow.

I left by train. I packed my giant suitcase and left Meadow behind to be collected by a social worker and returned to foster care. I knew, this was now over. I was numb as I sat on that platform, totally disconnected from the hustle happening around me. I was eloped in self-hatred. I totally blamed myself, despite knowing that deep down, this was not my fault.

Contact was immediately reduced to three hours a week and not long later, you guessed it, we were back at court.

The final hearing lasted 4 days I do believe. Me, mum, and nanny travelled to court every day that week, armed with nothing but the facts. Rashford was my representative that week. He had been there for our first ever court hearing, so he kind of knew how close I had been to success and that the doctors had been on my side, but he didn't seem enthusiastic at all, but I know now that he already knew it didn't matter, they adoption was already in place.

Prior to court, I had been given some paperwork to look through. In that paperwork was a stunning back and white picture of Meadow with a little caption underneath detailing her name, why she was available for adoption (mum is mentally ill) and what she likes.

Before the adoption had been agreed, weeks before, whilst I was still at the unit, they had added my baby to the baby catalogue. The book of babies for people to adopt. She was placed on a page, selling her story to the highest bidder.

I was absolutely disgusted, and I confronted them about it. The reply was always the same, *'we parallel plan so if the adoption is granted the child has a new home to go to rather than staying in care long term.'* It seems the most logical answer, but it is also absolute corruption at its finest.

Imagine seeing your child up for sale in the Argos book. Imagine how sick you'd have to be, to put an ad like that out there for a child, whose mother was still in court fighting for them. That's not helping the child, that's assuming the child is your commodity, an object to be obtained. It's like moving furniture into a house while the old tenants are still sleeping in their bed.

There comes a point when you start to feel like you're going crazy. Your thoughts will darken at the most unexpected times and in chilling ways. You'll begin to question if you ever really knew the meaning of hatred until now; standing there, behind the person stealing your child, whilst a hammer lays on the table just to your right & the urge to bring it down on the back of their wretched protruding skull threatens to overtake you.

My fingers twitch involuntarily of me a few times. I noticed how grey she was getting, how her hair was starting to thin, this frail hag had more power than anyone else in the building, even the judge.

I wondered what kind of weird yelp noise she'd make when the hammer made impact with her head.

I feel him next to me. The table between us suddenly feels so small. I don't want to talk right now. I wish mum would stop pulling my coat. I'm so close I could just...

I turn & smile at the reception boy who seems to bat for female attention where he can & carry on with my day. I avoid the lift and take the stairs. The proximity was threatening to turn me feral. I guess it's not just the lion that roars when its cub is in danger, the human subconscious does too.

I've wished on so many eleven, elevens
that they became hours
and I've wished on so many shooting stars
that suns have lived and died.

I've pondered on so many thoughts
that I've taken them into my dreams
and I've wondered how to tell you why
yet, after all these light-years and moments that I've lived,
I still have no answers.

Chapter Twelve

Those 4 days were long and quite frankly a waste of time. I sat and listened as the 2 medical doctors, the court had ordered, gave evidence, largely in my favour, just to have the whole row of the LA audibly tut the whole way through.

I watched Edith and her solicitor, elbow each other and smiling when Dr Dru predicted I'd continue to have more babies until I was allowed to keep one. Their action is what led me to abort my next pregnancy and then seek a sterilisation. They were not hiding their joy in removing more babies from me in the future.

 My mother had a seizure on the stand. Not an ounce of empathy was shown, they just rushed off for an early lunch refusing to even help fetch first aid, while I struggled to hold my mother up, so she didn't come crashing down off the podium.

I sat and listened to lies told about me. I watch the hyena and her pack wink and smile at one another and scowl at me if I made eye contact. It was obvious and clear emotional abuse, and the judge did nothing. But we knew the judge was friends with the guardian. How?

I received my contact papers and other forms to go through with my lawyer, Irene, before court. A total waste of an hour's appointment. She shot down any issues I had. Nanny commented to me afterward that *'she didn't seem to want to help you very much dear.'*

 On the back pages we noticed some emails between Edith and some of the previous judges we had met and some we did not know but where able to google.

They were arranging to meet on a Sunday for cricket, a picnic and to discuss cases. It was in black and white that these judges were not impartial, and cases were being discussed outside working hours and venues.

We showed these to Irene on the day and she tore them and balled them into the bin, stating it was an accident and not important. The person supposedly fighting to stop the LA getting my child, was disposing of ground-breaking hard evidence of personal and professional causes colliding. I wish I'd taken photocopies, but I didn't and now I have nothing but my word on this.

My time came to take the stand. I'm still proud, to this day, of how well I did. I kept myself together quite well considering.

The LA lawyer would ask me the same questions over and over but word it differently each time. Very quickly I began to respond with *'you just asked me that, I've answered twice, I will not answer again.'* My response was greeted with some awkward laughter from around the room. They thought me stupid, like I could be tricked into answering differently from the truth I already spoke. It's demeaning. It was also very clear that the way Rashford was asking questions of people was not the same. He had zero intention of tripping them up, he was there to save face. I wish I had represented myself, but I didn't know I had the option.

We had to return the following week for the judgment we already knew was going to be made. So back to court we went, just to hear the judge declare the adoption granted. She stamped her papers and they all got up to leave like the bell for recess just went off. I no longer existed to them. I no longer had a child. I was just another person in the same building as these state sanctioned child traffickers.

I had 2 more contacts left. My regular one that week and then the final one. Me and mum attended together the regular one. Meadow was a little bit tired and fretful and spent the hour just laying on my chest dozing and babbling quietly to me and my mum. It was a lovely hour for the 3 of us, despite what we knew would come. So, I never went back for that final goodbye.

It was a bold and controversial move. Lacey tried to convince me I'd regret it and even tried to indicate Meadow would hate me for it later, but I did not relent. Our final contact had been pleasant and peaceful, as opposed to the horrific distress of my previous kid's final contact. I maintain to this day; it was the right choice for me

76

and Meadow. It was not a choice I made on a whim for my own selfish needs.

I never got to see Meadow or Freya have their first birthdays, steps, words, or anything beyond, not even a Xmas. Some other women got to have all those moments. Moments I'd dreamed of from the day I saw 2 lines staring back at me. They had come and gone in a flash.

A few weeks later I found out I was pregnant again. Very unexpected indeed. It was with great sadness and reluctance; I had a termination. I attended the hospital to take my pill and spent several hours reliving the memories of birth, to pass a horrific mass with a small but recognisable baby. I've never recovered from that.

During the aftermath of me losing Meadow and having a termination, I once again had my time to grieve stolen from me. West made a serious suicide attempt after I refused to let him keep living with me when he had a flat of his own. Afterall, we were separated at this point and I was seeing someone else.

I got a call from the hospital. It was nearly midnight, but West had managed to call himself an ambulance after slashing his wrist. He needed surgery and lost a lot of blood.

I went to see him the next day to ask what occurred although I already knew a lot of it was about getting me to unblock his calls and tend to him.

He was whiter than I'd ever seen a living person. There was no doubt he really had been shaking hands with the reaper just a few hours before.

A nurse appeared to do his vitals. She honed in on me immediately. Clearly West had been telling her all about his version of me.

She loudly chastised me for not being there for my husband and him having to take up space in an NHS bed because I wouldn't let him come home with me and care for him. She belittled me and asked me what I thought I was doing being so neglectful to this sick man.

I explained that West and I had been separated for almost 2 years at that point and we did not live together and it was not my place to care for him if he was a risk to himself.

She informed me I was very wrong as we were still legally tied and then called me abusive. West lay in the bed looking flustered, he had not expected his tail of woe to come out as a form of attack, just seconds after he had manipulated me into compliance.

I was furious. I informed him, in front of her, I was leaving and not returning, I had the loss of a child to keep me busy. Several nearby patients exclaimed shock out loud, it was clear only half a story was being told but this did nothing to stem the nurses view that I was an abusive and neglectful wife.

Perhaps if I'd not been so wrapped in my own decaying mind, I'd have had the courage to stand up and tell her to keep her beaky nose out of what she didn't know.

Within a week, another doctor talked me into collecting West and taking him home. Why they could not transfer him to the psych ward I do not know. I ended up with him staying at my home for months because he claimed he was to traumatised to return to his home.

It was me who had to clean the horrific blood-soaked scene that he had left behind. I am traumatised by that to this day and my phobia of blood all started there. I can't tolerate a blood test without feeling faint now. Not only did he steal my grief, but he caused me more trauma with life changing consequences. Eventually I felt trapped enough to agree to work on the marriage. Grief makes us vulnerable and people exploit that.

Many months later, in the summer of 2010, I was invited to meet Meadow's adoptive parent. I knew roughly from the previous time what to expect. A chat, a chance for them to stare at you and gauge what their new baby will look like one day and a picture op, all of you standing together pretending to be besties. It's an awkward process for all involved so credit to the birth parents and adopters who take the time to do this.

When a child is adopted, the LA like to make a 'life story book' with pictures and info about the birth family for the child to have when they turn 18. We provided a ton of pictures for Freya and Jay's book. I was also told I could write about their births and other things like a poem. We had given the pictures and were told we could bring the rest in the following week and see the book itself. But when we went back the book had 'already gone.' So, we have no idea what it says or contains. I never saw Meadow's book either.

 I spent many years wondering what they adopters must have thought of us. What had they even been told? Half truths at best. I got the distinct sense Jay and Freya's adoptive mother would rather have been eating dung than sat there talking to us, however her husband was more involved, and we got a little sense of who he was. When we met them, we were given a picture of the kids. This would be the only picture we ever got.

We were informed they were changing Freya's name but did not say what to. This left a boiling rage inside me, but I just smiled politely. I chose that name with purpose.

We chatted a while and West and I managed to read between some lines when the adoptive father made some blunders about their location. As a result, we knew our kids would be about an hours' drive away. They would still be right under our nose and so close but so far.

The day of meeting Meadow's adopter, Cheryl, it was a lovely June afternoon which added a sense of cheeriness to the proceedings. The adopter was a single woman, well into later years I'd wager from her grey hair and fine lines, who had already adopted a little boy a few years previously. She was nice enough, of what I was allowed to gather.

I think Meadow's adopter was told not to talk too much and limit conversation. She paused to think before every answer she gave. She seemed nice but it felt like she was trying to recall a script as opposed to showing me her true self, so I have no idea who my child is being raised by. I don't know where or have any clues. Meadow is nothing but a memory for me now.

I was never given a picture this time. I'd been far to assumptive believing that would happen. I was also told I'd not be getting any in the letters, like I had requested, as many other mums got them, because Meadow was a *'distinctive looking child.'*

And that was it. The end of my war with social services and the family courts.

Again, I was left with no help going forward. Just a letterbox contract which the adoptive mother never actually signed.

I asked for support or places I could contact for help dealing with this loss and I was told that they don't have connections to those sorts of agencies. Social services don't work with agencies that help birth families deal with their loss! Let the magnitude of that irony sit in the apex of your heart for just a moment and feel the coldness of that.

It's also worth noting that writing letters is not a legal contract and the adopters can opt out of that at anytime they like and not keep the contact open between you and your child, effectively enabling them to do a vanishing act and pretend you never existed.

We used to be able to send birthday cards as well as a letter to Freya and Jay, but we were asked to stop because 'the adoptive parents were finding it difficult!!' Not the kids, not me, the woman who birthed them and stays in bed and cries on their birthday every year, but the adopters were finding it hard. The audacity had me and West riled, but we complied, desperate to make sure they kept the letters up and they did until about 2 years ago, when they stopped for seemingly no reason.

Chapter Thirteen

It's been well over a decade since all this happened. Yet I still suffer the lasting impact of the unfair permanent separation and unjust adoption of my children.

Years of therapy have not even scratched the surface of this trauma. It is only in writing this book, I have really begun to deal with the impact this has had on me long term. It has caused me more pain that any other abuse or traumatic situation I have lived through and there's been many.

I cannot speak for my children, my family, or anyone else who may have been affected by my kid's adoption, I can only speak for me, and this loss has been a pure torture that has never left me.

To this day I have problems trusting people, especially my own family. I have a constant wall up around me and as a result live mostly in isolation with very few friends. It borders paranoid at times.

Meeting new people and doing new things is a source of misery. I never know what I am meant to say as a birth mother. Do I tell the story to this stranger and hope they don't dismiss me, or do I live life as a fraud and carry my babies like a secret shame?

I can no longer access certain types of care for my wellbeing due to the continued mistreatment of me by the mental health team, since the loss of my kids. I no longer feel safe with them. I've continued to have diagnosis after diagnosis and zero consistency. For 10 years I was denied medication and support for my mental health and I firmly believe this was an attempt to keep me unwell so they could take babies from me in the future.

I have a lot of anger; this is often perceived by professionals and authority as me being defiant or antisocial. I can be quite bitter about pregnancy in other women too.

I am terrified of children, avoiding them at all costs. This has severed many friendships and sabotages my ability to bond with my stepdaughter. I constantly feel like my mere presence is damaging to any child near me. This is the narrative the LA have drummed into the grooves of my brain.

My problems with depression continued to grow in severity over the years often seeing me lost in a dissociated state on my bed for days at a time. I've faced financial issues, unable to keep a job due to my chaotic inability to manage these depressive episodes.

As times gone on, I have developed social anxiety and hardly leave the house. I feel judged and afraid, like I am standing on the podium again, soaked in milk.

I have flashbacks, emotional and visual, especially of my last contact with Jay and Freya. This has been linked to me developing Functional Neurological Disorder which includes seizures and other life altering neurological phenomena. The belief is that the brain is converting deep emotional stress into physical manifestations; also known as conversion disorder. My symptoms began a few months after the loss of Meadow. This unjust and cruel separation and caused me much physical and mental harm and still I could not get any answers or support until many years later in 2017.

I have almost zero self-belief and confidence and I doubt everything I do. I often find I believe I'm useless and my existence is meaningless. I'm so self-loathing. Even when I do deserve praise, I am suspicious of any positive feedback.

I blamed myself and allowed myself to fall into one toxic situation after another believing I deserved nothing but misery. I was forever pushing people away to 'keep them safe,' because I truly believed I must be some kind of animal to be treated as I had. I guess I still push people away but now it's become about protecting me.

I have an emotional melt down every month with my period. It took me five years to convince the doctor I wanted to be sterilised. I was so scared of facing the agony of another loss, and subjecting my wonderful husband, Michael, to such a loss that I cut off my ability to be a mum completely. Every month, I still monitor ovulation and secretly hope I'll have a miracle conception because the brutal truth is, I didn't choose to make an irreversible decision like this because I didn't want to be a mum again. I did it because I felt I had no choice, because no matter who I am or what good I do, the LA want to take what's rightfully mine.

I've been in a psychological war with the LA this whole time. I can't express the impact this has truly had. The ripple effect runs a very deep ravine within me.

You might wonder how I ever got to that point in my life, especially so young. All this occurred before I was 23. That needs a whole book of its own, but I think a breakdown of information relevant to this situation is in order.

I was homeless when I met West as a teen. We both ended up in hostels and me unexpectedly pregnant. We had a rushed marriage. We were offered a two bedroom home away from my hometown and family and told if we refused it, we'd not be granted another option and I'd have to live in a mother and baby unit alone until another house come up. We now know they say this to pressure you and if we'd held out, we'd probably have had our one demand met, to stay in our home town with family support.

The day I gave birth to Jay was the day we were meant to move in. I ended up spending the first five days in hospital with him which was hard for me.

The first few months of Jay's life was ok. I had depressive episodes still but managed to remain functional whilst working closely with mental health and using medication. My episodes were shorter at this point in my life, and this is reflected in paperwork I have since had from the mental health team and attributed to the medication I was using at the time.

Over those two short years I'd be diagnosed with: postnatal depression, Tourette's, ADHD and then Bipolar. It was very confusing to be told one thing after another.

Having a baby opened my eyes somewhat. I suddenly had a child, who I needed to protect from all the dark things in the world, I had had the misfortune to come across. The magnitude of that task was not lost on me. For the first time, I was realising what had happened to me was very wrong.

I spent those early days cleaning the house, sterilising bottles, and cooking. West was not working, he insisted he needed to stay home and care for me because he deemed that I was somewhat woefully incompetent. So, West would watch tv and hold Jay who slept most of the day. Eventually West said I needed to stop cleaning so much and spend time with the baby. So, I did, and the mess quickly became overwhelming.

I do tend to stress clean, it's not unfair to assume this was me avoiding the overwhelm of suddenly been thrown into full adulthood alongside my trauma surfacing.

West then began to make friends nearby and it wasn't long before cannabis was brought back into our lives. Within months, not only did we have West's drinking addiction to afford but a double drug addiction and a child to provide for. By the time Jay was a year old, I was struggling with depression and feeling unmotivated, and drained.

I reached out to the health visitor because I was struggling to manage my mood and the fact was, we were living in poverty at this point. She referred us with consent to the LA for assistance.

A social worker called Heather was assigned and she wasn't the worst. She liaised with the mental health team and often gave us food parcels and vouchers. However West often used appointments to talk about how bad my mental health was and how he was struggling to care for us both. He made himself to be a victim in as many ways as he could, and this is what drew so much scrutiny to me. He had managed to convince me I was seriously ill and needed lifelong care.

He would greet Heather with major statements like 'she hit me.' Always skipping to the cataclysmic event and leaping over the full story. One time he hit me back and managed to convince me and Callum that it was my fault! I had caused him to react, but my reactions were my own.

Don't get me wrong, I am responsible for my actions. I knew giving him a slap was not going to solve anything, I just saw red and exploded before I could catch myself. I did reach out for help with this behaviour, which I'll discuss in a bit, I truly believe my environment was the cause of this aggressiveness, as now, with West totally absent from my life and me being in a healthy marriage, there is no pending issues. I accept my role, but I do not accept I chose to act out of malice rather that I reacted from fear.

I recall one day I was tidying the kitchen and I opened a cupboard, and it was stuffed full of empty cider bottles. I asked West about it, and he said they must have been in there for months. I didn't think anything of it until a few weeks later, when I found more in there, and in the wardrobe, shed and airing cupboard. I confronted him again and he accused me of spying and overreacting to create a problem to distract from me being an abuser. I'd confront him with evidence, and he would still turn it around on me.

Another time, we were arguing as we were all getting ready to go to see Heather. Jay was refusing to sit in his pushchair, fretful from the tension building around him. I told him off, raising my voice slightly and as I did so I pointed my finger at him and said 'no.' As I did, I accidently poked his face as he thrashed about in temper. He wasn't hurt and continued to defy me as expected of a small child. But West saw it out the corner of his eye and decided I had slapped Jay. I maintained that I had not, it was an accidental poke, and West was already angry and creating issues where there was none. He told the social worker what I had done, and Jay had to be checked head to toe for bruises. We were lucky they hadn't taken him there and then.

No signs of any harm were found, and the issue was dismissed but it left even further scrutiny to fall on me. Every time they saw us, West had another tale of woe. Whatever it was he was trying to achieve; he built the case for removal of our kids. Maybe if he'd known that, he'd have been less histrionic about every disagreement we had. To this day you can't confront West about anything without him making it about his victimhood.

A strong memory of my behaviour towards West that sticks with me was the time I just hit West before the argument started.

I was cooking spag bol, out of nowhere he stormed into the kitchen and began to shout about me tutting "what's your problem now, Annie." I explained I had spilt something.

He came over to the oven and began regurgitating his putrid breath and hatred all over me and waving his finger in my face, so I just slapped him. As I said earlier, the situation only resolved once I reacted violently, so I ended the situation before it started. He was stunned. He stormed back out saying "I can't believe you did that Annie, you're sick, I didn't do anything to you."

I continued to cook dinner. I then calmly took our dinner through and sat down to eat. Jay was watching TV in his highchair and there was no need to fight anymore.

"Why are you being nice to me, Annie?" West said a few minutes later.

"You're my husband why wouldn't I be?

"You hit me, Annie!"

" Like you said, you did nothing wrong so now I'm being nice to you. Sorry for hitting you" I looked at him, smiled and turned back to the TV. West began to rage. Jay turned around and made a screaming sound. I wasn't sure if he was mocking West or telling him to shut the hell up because his TV shows were on but a let a giggle escape me and hat escalated things.

"You are turning my own son against me, Annie, you are sick!" I put my food aside. The smell of his cider breath was threatening to eject the contents of my stomach. He literally made me feel sick. Our son was not yet a year old and he wasn't my outburst he was reacting too.

I walked into the kitchen having given up eating. West was still screaming about how he did nothing wrong and how I was now being nice. He slammed the kitchen door closed, locking me in the kitchen with him and leaving our small son unattended in his highchair. I pointed this out and loudly told him to keep the door open. He accused me of trying to argue in front of Jay to turn his son on him.

 There was no winning this one. I messed up when I reacted to soon. The end result of me hitting him wasn't what he had been seeking all this time. He was seeking to fight with me, to have a chance to scald and belittle me, make accusations, and further conduct narcissistic abuse on me. It was all becoming so clear.

 I told Heather about this incident and how Jay had been left alone because of how West had behaved, and nobody battered an eye. If West had said I had done that, I'd have been given another tearing down, sent to the psychiatrist about my behaviour and told I needed to attend parenting classes *(which they never actually produced for me)* But West, again, managed to make himself the hero and me the villain.

My mother-in-law, Sally, is supposed to be here to offer a bit of support and family time. Instead, I now have 2 people stripping away at my sanity. The coach journey was long, and Jay is crying in his pram. He's hungry but rather than stop and feed him, Sally insists we walk home quickly and feed him there. So, I push the pram. I speed walk with the hopes of encouraging everyone else to speed up. After 10 minutes of solid screaming and being stared at by passers-by, I feel like a bomb ready to detonate into screams. I can hear West and Sally talking, they are a few feet behind me on the path. I stop in my tracks, step aside and walk away from the pram, knowing they are right there to take over.

West flips. He starts screaming down the road at me for 'leaving Jay on the side of the road alone.' I know that's not what happened at all and I speed up my pace more. I cannot breathe. I can't even see straight there's so many tears in my eyes. I am totally worn out from a week of West and Sally taking bites out of me.

Sally feeds Jay his bottle. West comes upstairs where I am unpacking Jay's things.

He is screaming in my face, spit settling on my skin and the smell of tramp juice making my stomach curdle. All my life, men who have sexually and physically assaulted me have had alcohol on their breath. The smell turns my muscles to steel, my blood to ice and my brain sears as though it's on fire. He's telling me I'm sick and need help and insists they were so far behind he had to run to get the pushchair before someone else did. I know they were less than 10ft away, I am convinced but he works very hard to change my mind for me.

I blow! A throw a heavy white candle across the room and it hurtles through the glass of my son's bedroom window. Now I've messed up. West smirks at me and tells me 'You'll regret that, Annie.'

I had no idea that the type of behaviour West was exhibiting was abuse. I'd grown up abused, to me this was just how people treated me so when professionals asked me my view, I'd comply that I was out-of-control and almost intolerable to live with.

Jay was placed on the child protection register and we were fine with that. We continued regular visits with Heather, and they paid for Jay to attend a childminder once a week to give me and West both a chance to deal with things. West was always saying he never had time for him due to the struggle of caring for us both, so he was granted that time. He used that time to clean and drink cider, singing loudly and angering the neighbours and giving me yet another headache rather than attending addiction counselling or men's support groups.

A point came when I was sent to live with my maternal grandparents. I was there a couple of months. I saw Jay at a contact centre twice a week with Ursula and my grandparents and it was fine. No assessments were done, it was just a neutral place to see Jay as me and West were not talking.

During that time, I had no observable angry outburst or deep depression. I did not lay in bed staring into the void in a dissociative state once. Like that time in the ward, the problem was gone. I was

89

having a social life again and Jay came to spend a weekend with me. I took him out alone and we had a great time.

I moved back home. My grandparents never liked having me around too long unless there was money.

I was signed up for anger management with my CPN. After a few sessions, and West complaining I'd come home even 'angrier than before,' it was stopped because it was seen to be exacerbating the issue. I recall flipping at this and aggressively shoving West in the waiting room. The only help I had was being removed. I was heavily criticised for doing this in front of my son.

Eventually things settled and I was pregnant again and Jay removed from the CPR and the LA stopped aiding us. Things were fine with the pregnancy apart from my struggling mental state as I have previously discussed in earlier chapters. Nothing was wrong until the day the LA came back in the new year, and physically barged in and up the stairs to look at our home and check our child for any signs of abuse.

I was home alone at the time with Jay. West was out with his friends. Callum knocked on the door, I answered, and he literally pushed heavily pregnant me aside and ran up my stairs. I was confused and frightened. This man had unexpectedly turned up and barged into my home.

I had been cleaning that day. As always, when I did a good clean, I found endless empty cider bottles. So, when Callum went into our bedroom, he was greeted with about 6 bin liners of rubbish, mostly consisting of blue plastic. However, Jay's room, although very basic with no carpet, half decorated and furniture older than me, was clean and secure.

Callum stood at the top of the stairs looking down at me, seemingly deflated the bathroom was clean and came flying past me into the lounge. He complained there was a pile of stuff behind the armchair and I had not yet folded the washing, then headed to the kitchen.

Anyone who knows me will tell you I hate washing up. So, West's only chore was to wash up. As usual, for him that meant, washing up what he needed to use at the time and leaving the rest for days or longer. On this occasion, there were plates piled high with rotting food.

I asked Callum if he now believed me about West's drinking, but he proceeded to tell me our home was not fit for purpose, and he'd be back in a few days to make sure we'd bought it up to scratch. This included completing the décor in Jay's room, which was started by the previous tenant.

Jay is sat between my legs on his bed ready for his bedtime story. This is our time every day, just us.
My ever-growing stomach provides a solid back rest for him and as time goes on I wonder how he can sit so curved.
We read the same story every night. It's so routine he now knows when to chime in with the special word, 'yellow.'
We follow my finger under each word of wobble bear's adventure. This is my favourite time of day.

I don't deny that social services did offer some support in the early stages. Time is very precious as a parent and those few hours a week with the childminder mattered a great deal. But no one, across all those services in our lives, managed to spot the emotional abuse of a young woman, isolated with her alcoholic husband. As a matter of fact, I was often blamed. My marriage to West has left me with permanent life changing emotional damage.

So where did it go wrong? The key difference is that our first referral was us reaching out, but the next time it was the damning call they'd had from our own family. I still don't know what was said but it must have been awful.

I know some of them considered our home vile with its laundry piles, damp walls and mismatch furniture. It was basic but we had what we needed. Jay had a variety of clothing, toys, books and more. He was always fed, entertained, and clothed. He had eczema and we treated that best we could. There were times we went hungry to make sure he ate. Pasta was like air for me and West.

Not once did my family roll up their sleeves and offer help with the house or come visit, instead they turned on me in the worst way. It was always easier to pass me to someone else when I became too much bother. This is how I ended up in care myself.

A mix of poorly managed mental health, unacknowledged addiction and domestic abuse ushered our little family into a nightmare.

As for my use of cannabis, I would like to state I attended a local drug service and was told they don't help with cannabis as it's only psychologically addictive.

I do not deny I had my issues and so did West. I asked for help so many times, each time more desperate but the wrong things were dealt with. I do not believe we deserved to be cruelly ripped apart and forever denied a right to provide for and love our children. More could have been done to keep us together and as for Meadow, there is absolutely no justification for the permanency of that removal given all the previous issues were no longer the actual issue. And it was definitely not ok for them to be able to hold the threat of removing all my future offspring.

My chest adorns heavy armour
it presses my sternum into collapse,
metal moulding to my ribs,
lungs mashed, and heart fisted.

War is over
but the casualty still bleeds beneath the medals.

Chapter Fourteen
So, what's the motive?

Why would social workers behave in such a way to gain children for adoption? I think that's the most valid question in this book and although I have no definite answer, there are several theories as to why this is happening. I shall detail them below. Please bear in mind, I don't necessarily agree to them all as facts, but I receive with an open mind. Ultimately unless the corrupt individuals involved decide to 'fess up, we may never know.

1. **Cash bonuses to get kids out of long-term care and into permanent homes.** In the year 2000, the labour government bought in an incentive where the LA get a bonus every time they find a permanent home for a child. This was done with the hope that older children may find adoptive homes rather than continuing to be a drain on the by the system and be moved about continuously. But no one wants to adopt a child of five, ten or fifteen, so to meet these set targets and obtain financial gain, the family courts and LA began to create permanent homes for babies in care, babies who did not need to be in care. They essentially exploited a system designed to do genuine good. Not only do they take new-borns based on predictions, but they also leave actual vulnerable kids to rot in the system. Please note, if you are an adopter or hoping to adopt one day and you only want an infant, you are part of the problem.

MP Tim Yeo was very outspoken about this and spent time talking to victims of the LA and trying to raise this in parliament. So yes, government officials are aware, and have been a while, that this is not working. Social workers went to the newspapers about it back in 2007. I have been informed this policy is no longer in place and was abolished in 2013 due to this exploitation, however on searching for confirmation, I was not yet able to find it. They continue to remove children to upkeep their figures and meet targets and give the illusion of success.

Afterall, a successful department gets funding. It is also worth noting, not all financial gains would be documented. Under table cash exchange is also a likely practice.

2. **Genetic testing and rhesus negative blood.** One of the scariest things in my situation is not knowing where my kids are. If my kids had died, I'd know their tiny bodies were safe in the ground and their soul in some ethereal place. But as it is, I have no idea of their fate.

I once had someone message on social media about a report they were handing in to police, evidencing children were being taken by the LA in this country, for genetic testing in Dubai and they were especially interested in people with rhesus negative blood, which me, and likely my kids, all have.

Whether this is true, or speculation is another matter, but one can't help but wonder if there's some truth to it, especially on account of rhesus negative blood being rare and linked to everything from aliens to preventing disease. That, coupled with the fact I was denied pictures of my kids, unlike most other parents, makes it a frightening possibility that they are not in a nice adoptive home at all. Where's the proof really? The letter's I get could be written by anyone.

3. **Adoption is a billion-pound industry across the planet.** Hopeful adopters spend thousands to adopt a child through an agency such as the LA. People who want to adopt are very likely to be wealthy people of middle class and up, whereas birth parents tend to be lower class. To keep these people spending money, adoption agencies must keep finding babies to sell.

With abortion legal in many places and contraception easier to obtain, there have been less unwanted babies than a few decades ago. So, they create issues among the vulnerable groups to secure adoption for the highest available bidder.

Given that some of the biggest states in America, notably Texas, have now banned abortion, means there will be more young parents forced to give up their babies to adoption. So, the cycle continues and the adoption industry thrives.

Unfortunately, most people adopt because they WANT a baby, it's nothing to do with what a child NEEDS.

4. **Psychological experiments/study.** Given how many of the birth parents are treated during and after this process and the fact that adoptees are four times more likely to commit suicide, it's fair to say the psychological impact of adoption is a given obvious. But what if they torture the most vulnerable of us just to see how we react.

In the 1960s a psychologist named Kentler placed foster teen boys in homes with convicted paedophiles, knowing they would likely be abused. His thinking was that the sex offenders may change or still be able to parent. So, they used nonconsenting children and young people, with no parent to advocate for them, to see if this would work. This is just one of many unethical experiments conducted on children in the care system.

What's to say unethical practices are still not occurring. With no physical contact going forward, how do I know my kids are not being subjected to abuse or therapy to continue to monitor the effects of early separation or something else. There are far too many cases of adopters abusing their child, this I have witnessed with my own eyes.

5. **Social distribution.** This is a class divide tactic. In order to change our social structure long term and reduce the burden of poverty on the system, children from lower class families are being redistributed to the upper class in an attempt to alter their upbringing and prospects in life and therefore the type of people we have in our world going forward (working and upper class) you could just provide better prospects to kids in poverty but that would be a

financial burden on the system. The LA do not like to spend money where possible which is the motive to not fund keeping families together but move children on to someone who is self sufficient and not in need of aid.

6. **Increased cases of infertility mean increased demand for adoptable children.** Since world WW2 infertility has become a much bigger issue in our society. Often hopeful adopters decide to adopt as a last resort, after IVF has failed. It's rarely a first choice in family building and that's an issue. The adoption industry is allowing people struggling with infertility to believe adoption is the answer to infertility trauma and their need for a child, regardless of the consequences. Adoption is rarely exclusively about a child's needs. This constant demand, which people are willing to pay thousands to have met, gives adoption agencies and social workers incentive to remove children for redistribution. Infertility is a deeply saddening thing to face but it does not entitle anyone to someone else's child.

-

A lot of the tactics used by the LA are parallel to those used by emotional abusers. Below are some of those behaviours and examples of them in my own case. If a partner did this to you, it would now be called domestic abuse and you'd be considered a victim.

1. **Isolation** by severing contact with West and not allowing me to meetings while in the psych ward was isolation. Sending me to the assessment unit and cutting off visits for 4 weeks without warning was another example. The psychologists said this would be DAMAGING to me and they did it anyway.

Family courts also have 'gagging orders' which forbid you to discuss your case with anyone, including family or a therapist, on risk of prison. This leaves you emotionally isolated.

2. **Manipulation and lies** are seen throughout. One such example is from West's time in the b&b. Whilst there the owner told him the place was going under and they would likely be closing soon as he was struggling to care for his wife. Within 2 years of our kids' case, the b&b did not close, but instead built an extension and increased business and the woman put in a top care home. We firmly believe he was paid for his statement to the court, which he stated that Jay was *'deranged'* because he had wet the bed. Jay was 2 years old, had little stability at that time and had been potty training.

I believe a lot of money exchanged hands under tables to get people like this and the foster carer to say things that helped secure the case for adoption. Again, his desperation to not lose his livelihood would have been a great incentive.

Just before Meadow and me went away, I was granted a two-bedroom home from the council. They called the LA as I said Meadow was currently in care and Lacey told them not to let me have the house as the baby 'would not be coming home.' One of the things they wanted was for me to no longer be living in an upstairs single room flat, but they made sure I did not have the solution in time for the final court hearing.

3. **Gaslighting** leaves you doubting your reality and sanity. When I raised West's drink issue I was often greeted with *'and what about you? Or told 'he's not that bad.'* I was always made to feel I was the problem, and my concerns were just my hysterical nature. West used to use this tactic on me regularly.

4. **Threats and intimidation** by bringing section 21s to me. There was a time Lacey gave me some forms to fill out for

Meadow's vaccinations. A section 21 was on the back, and she felt the need to point this out to me and tell me *'You can rip that off.'* She was letting me know she can trick me if needs be.

5. **Hearsay** is stating something with no physical proof. They claimed I left a voicemail threatening to kill my unborn child but could not ever produce this tape. What if that had been needed for a criminal case? What happened to that vital evidence?

I also asked Irene to point out that a lot of the contact notes were very subjective, and these people never get called in to court to confirm they ever wrote it, but she would not feel it relevant. A great deal of the LA's evidence is pure hearsay and would be dismissed in a criminal court.

6. **Stonewalling and withholding information**! Karen refusing to answer questions in court was the most outrageous stonewalling I have ever seen. The LA often ignored my calls, for example early in my pregnancy with Meadow and refused to help us with the FCC.

7. **Humiliation** by allowing me to continue for hours in court while soaked in breast milk, police presence at the birth of Freya, laughing at me in court and belittling me for not breastfeeding are just a few examples.

8. **Groom and befriend** was something they started executing on me during my own time in care. In this case it was done by telling me I'm a good mummy to my face then criticizing me in the contact notes.

Callum told me the section 21 I signed in hospital was so he could 'help me,' but it was done to gain my trust. Remember, he used my concerns about West to trick me into believing he saw it too and wanted to help. He took my desperation and warped it.

99

9. **Trivializing**. The FGC effort was dismissed, our evidence not raised in court, and the psychologist's advice ignored. They trivialised anything we bought to the table.
10. **Stereotyping** by assuming abused children will be abusers and mentally ill people can't parent is assumptive and based in stereotype.
11. **Baiting** was often used in the court room. Opening the window and smiling right at me, soaked through and cold, knowing any reaction would be used against me, was typical baiting. This is another one West used a lot. Baiting is what leads to 'reactive abuse.' **This is when a victim lashes out toward the abuser in response to the abuse. However, the abuser then shifts the blame on to their victim and accuses them of being the abuser themselves and often gains sympathy from external sources as a result.**
12. **Confusion** by denying me paperwork before court cases, not explaining my BPD diagnosis or what they wanted from me in the FGC all played a factor in not being able to adequately defend myself.

It's absurd to deny that underhand tactics were used to convince the court of the LA's case for adoption. They exploited a vulnerable girl and used her abuse to build a case against her. I don't think for a second, they couldn't see West for what he was. They chose to be his flying monkeys. These abuse tactics are what have caused me so much psychological damage going forward.

Would I have been 'mentally ill' anyway? Yes. Given I exhibited issues with my mental wellness from childhood, sent to see a psychologist aged 4, who also failed to spot my abuse, it's safe to say I'd have had trauma of some form. However, I can clearly see I declined a great deal after the loss of my children. It wasn't until

2016 that I had a life changing experience that allowed me to start changing, by choice.
Either way, I did not deserve to be treated this way by the very services that should have protected me as a child and then helped me to parent better.

I am the face of rage suppressed
medicated by my shame.
I am the beast who'll take you down
for your fall I'll take claim.

I am the war; the dark sublime
you'll fight but you will lose.
I am the darkness hurling up your guilt
the hand that holds your noose.
I am the conjurer and if you let loose
I'll summon the people too.
We are the end, you won't survive
when justice comes for you.

I am warrior
I am the victor
I am the chains you bare.
I am the scribe
I am the truth
I am the one who dares.
I AM THE ONE WITH NOTHING TO LOSE!

Chapter fifteen
What did I do that's so bad?

Another thing I have never understood is WHY I have been treated so badly, especially going forward after the adoption has been granted. Below are some examples of other cases of people I have known and met that indicate the way I've been treated is indeed, unusually relentless. Please note all names are changed for privacy purposes.

1. Chloe had been raised in care her whole childhood. She spent a brief time in prison, was diagnosed with Bipolar and become pregnant with her child all before turning eighteen. Her child was removed for the most ridiculous reasons including active satanism. After the adoption, Chloe was allowed letters and a photo every year. She fell pregnant again after a few years. By this time, she had moved out of her hometown and had a new partner. The new social worker had trouble accessing previous files and did some digging. Eventually this led to Chloe being told her case was handled illegally. She chose not to act on this despite the support offered. The new child has a lifelong disability and Chloe has been an exceptional mum to her, despite her own childhood lacking a permanent and secure parental role. It would appear her new circumstances and environment had changed her. Her mental illness did not make her unable to parent a child with complex needs because mothers with mental health issues are still capable people. She was also allowed pictures of the child each year. I wish Chloe and her children all the best for the future.

2. Vicky was in court at the same time as I was with Meadow. She had been charged with neglect and the story made the local newspapers. Social workers had found her passed out on the couch, a dog chained to a radiator and a baby left crying in a crib stained with faeces. The child was removed and quite rightly so, clearly things were out of hand. Within

3 years Vicky would be pregnant again. She left the heroin addict she'd been married too and went on to have a healthy baby. She was allowed to keep this child, despite an actual criminal history of child neglect just a handful of years before. To say I was outraged was an understatement. She went on to have another child after this. I was NEVER charged with anything. Why was Meadow taken from me when mothers like this get second chances?

3. Sharon was a victim of domestic violence, and her 2 children were subjected to sexual abuse, which she did not know about. She immediately left the abusive partner on finding this out, but social services still removed the children and put them up for adoption. Sharon gets letters and pictures every year and is even allowed to send physical birthday gifts to her kids. After about 5 years she got pregnant again with her new partner. The LA have been involved but Sharon and her baby remain together at home. I wish Sharon and her little one all the best in their future.

4. Robin had his first child as a teen and the teenage mother moved away and never contacted him again. A short time later he got another teen girl pregnant. Around this time, Robin was also found guilty on child sex abuse allegations and was made to register as a sex offender. He went on to have 2 more children. Despite this, no involvement has been had to assure these children are not being exposed to sexual abuse.

5. Emily had two sons over five. Her relationship with their dad was unhealthy and the whole housing estate knew. One day, Emily stabbed her partner, in the hand, in front of her kids. She was arrested but as it was a first offence, she got a slap on the wrist and nothing more. They relationship ended and she would not let the kids see their dad. Social

services were called as the kids had been present at the incident, but this was a one-off meeting.

6. Kerry had 4 kids all aged 4-8. She was dating a man called Ben. When the LA were informed about this relationship, they removed the kids and sent them to live with their father (remember they are too old to be adoptable) She went to court to appeal custody and when told she could have her kids home, but she had to stop dating Ben, she outright refused and chose him over the kids. Ben had lost access to all his kids previously because he was a dangerous and violent man. Something I can attest to this as a fact as he physically assaulted me as a teen and tried to rape me when I was pregnant with Meadow. So, these kids stayed with their dad and she got to see them at weekends. Ben dumped her a few weeks later and now she was alone without her kids. Two years later she was pregnant again. Social services started her prebirth assessment at 8 weeks. At 16 weeks she aborted the baby because she could tell 'they are gonna take it away and I don't want to end up like you Annie!' She fell pregnant again within months and was allowed to keep her child.

Is it a postcode lottery? Luck of the draw with which social worker you get. Or is it outright corruption with such a devious intent we can't begin to imagine it? The truth is, I don't think we'll ever truly know, we can only speculate.

I cannot think of any reasonable cause to not let me have a single picture of my kids growing up. That hurts! I once asked the letterbox adoption team if they can ask Meadow's adoptive mum to have her draw a picture of herself. That was denied.

Take some of the above examples, deliberate acts of abuse and neglect, and compare to my case. Why have I been subjected to such extreme measures? If I am such a risk to my children, why do I pass DBS checks and have worked with disabled children since the court allowed these adoptions to take place? It does not feel like this was ever about child protection at all, it was about babies for profit.

Imagine my seething rage every time I watch another person like Vicky or Chris, have another baby, while I remain empty, feeling like my only purpose as a woman is just a whisper in the wind.

The salt on my wounds is never ending. Whenever I see a parent slap their kid in the street, a father call his son an idiot or a mother scrolling her phone while her child feeds itself milk, I want to explode in rage because I had my kids removed from me for far less. My son came to no harm. They can talk about *'risk of emotional harm'* all they like but the fact is, we all, including Jay, suffered emotional harm from the brutal separation of our family unit. As for the girls, there was no chance given whatsoever. It's been proven that infants being taken from their mother at birth is incredibly damaging to their development we don't even do it to animals and yet, the LA will never acknowledge that what they do is often worse than anything the parents they penalize have ever done.

I always knew I'd be a writer. As a child I'd lose myself in words, preferring to hide in a bush and write poetry rather than play with the other kids. I had this deep knowing I'd be an author one day and several teachers encouraged this talent in me. I thought I'd write a spooky story and a tragic tale of young love. Instead, I ended up writing this book.

Whether this book reaches one person, be it one of my kids or a social worker looking for the other side's story, I did what I came to do.

Chapter Sixteen
Common questions

- How have you coped with your loss all this time?

I haven't.

People always say to me that they'd never be able to live with the loss of their kids, they'd simply die. Don't you think I wanted to? I even tried. But the fact is, if I die, who's going to tell them the truth? If I kill myself off, will my kids consider that act as me abandoning them?

I did nothing wrong, and I know what has been done to us is wrong and I 'll choose life just to make sure my kids know that because they were not given up or left behind. I wanted them. No one wants them like I do.

Coping looks like disabling depression some days and other days it looks like too many gins or watching the same movies because they are familiar constants. Coping is a fallout symptom of grief and trauma.

- Do you still feel like a mum?

I am still a mum. Mother is not a person but an energy; a state of being. Mothering is ultimately an act of service to something beyond you and I am always in service to my kids. I am also a very good cat mummy.

- Did you deserve it? What do you think should have happened?

Everyone will form their own opinion on what should happen to other people, we are judgmental by nature, our ability to judge can save lives but we often misjudge.

No, I do not believe permanent separation from any of my 3 children was fair and I do not believe any LA involvement with Meadow would have been required.

I think if they'd been able to get me secure accommodation in my hometown away from West, I'd have left him within a year of marrying him and probably been a better-rounded adult as a result. But they chose to ignore me about what was happening and take his word only.

They chose the option they knew would fail when it came to successful reunification with Meadow. They purposely acted to secure her adoption. I'll say it with my dying breath.

I also think, the timescale is a cop out. I could have attended the therapy with my kids in my care, with family or in foster care a while longer. The only reason they use this is because they don't want to pay out for foster care when they could earn thousands instead via adoption fees. Not enough was done to preserve our family.

- So, is it all West's fault?

No. I realise I have not portrayed my ex-husband in the best light. I've not exactly painted myself as an angel either. It was only looking back and writing this book, I realised just how much damage his lies and behaviour caused. He continues his smear campaign against me and told the mother of his second son a few years back the kid's adoption was my fault because I was *'dangerous.'*

We both played a role, as did our families and the local authority. I believe we all could have improved how we handled things but, I feel, to this day, West has not changed his ways and the string of issues he has had in the aftermath of our marriage just shows he creates drama.

West is always quick to blame EVERYONE for what's happened to him in life, but he will never acknowledge his own role unless it will illicit sympathy or praise. He must be the victim and that mentality is what has lost him his marriage and access to all his kids.

I have made my mistakes and I have expressed many of them here in this book and will disclose more in my autobiography one day. But it should be noted that West is not alone responsible for the actions leading to our children's adoption.

- Do you like the adoptive parents?

I don't know them well enough to have an opinion. I do not blame them for this situation and believe they are likely as oblivious to the

108

fact of forced adoption as anyone else. I am grateful they are taking care of my kids.

Meadow's adoptive parent feels more attentive and personal in letters and asks questions relevant to Meadow's needs and interests such as medical info and info about the bio family. Obviously, I'd like direct contact with her but I must consider she does not at this time, but I believe she will have good intentions in the future for Meadow. It should certainly be observed that my anger is with the local authority and family courts, not the adopting party who simply thought they were getting a child in genuine need

- **Are you going to make contact when the kids are 18?**

I believe that should be a choice they make. I don't know what they have been told, they may think I left them or worse, harmed them. They may not want a relationship with me or need answers and I must live knowing this rejection may come. It's no one's fault but the corrupt services behind the adoption. I hold no future decision against my kids, but I hope they'll at least hear or read my side of the story. I can tell you by the time this goes to print, I will be officially in reunion with my eldest child' Jay and working hard to get Freya some contact as they also seek that. Meadow's whereabouts and desires remain a mystery.

- **What would you have done differently, or think should have been done?**

For starters I'd never have bothered with a lawyer and legal aid, I'd have advocated for myself. That aside, I really don't think I could do anymore than I already had with the knowledge and resources I had at the time.

As for being a mother, if I knew then what I know now, I'd have left West and started over, even if it meant sofa surfing with Jay. I believe that decision could have prevented much of what happened, but I was an 18-year-old child, who had been raised to think alcoholism was a given for fathers and that my mum's previous partner's daily put downs were true. I was very much a product of my environment and that is something I have since been able to change for myself. Change is possible with the right support.

I ask you this; if reunification is always the goal, why was there never an attempt to reunite us with Jay and Freya? As for Meadow, if reunification was the true goal, why, instead of letting us go live with family and be under a supervision order, did they send me to a placement they knew would fail? Adoption is the true goal!

I think varying services inability to spot the serious emotional abuse West was conducting on me is the biggest factor at fault in this situation. Just like my entire childhood, my screams for help fell on deaf ears and somehow, I became the villain of the story, as victims often do with mental abuse.

More could have been done to help me to function better in my life and be a better parent had the correct diagnosis and acknowledgement of my trauma come earlier in my son's life rather than many moons later in 2017.

I also think a residential assessment with Jay and Freya could have been ideal for us as a family unit. I don't think West could have kept up his charming victim pretence under extended observation.

I believe more could have been done in the first case to reunite us and absolutely no serious attempt of reunification was ever taken with Meadow.

- **If you really thought you were wronged, why didn't you appeal the adoptions?**

In the first kids' case, my lawyer told me that I couldn't appeal the adoption (I asked as soon as the decision was made) I was a naive 20-year-old kid who never thought for a second MY lawyer would lie to me.

In the third child's case, I again asked immediately, but the same lawyers told me that this time I could but there was no legal aid available and I 'd have to pay extortionate court costs over years of fighting. She made it sound as impossible as she could. Again, I now know I was lied to. My own lawyer sabotaged my cases.

Epilogue

As I sit here writing this, realising I am almost done with reliving my adoption agony, I notice the xmas tree lights twinkling. My stepdaughter's presents sit under the tree and yet every time I look at it, I can only think of my kids. Another xmas without them. This pain is never ending. It's in every holiday, walk around the park and back to school photo on social media, I can't escape.

People are always quick to judge, especially on the internet. Thank you for caring enough about the facts to read this book. Given you have endured my version of the story, you may have formed your own view on whether I deserved to be permanently separated from all 3 of my beautiful babies, possibly forever.

I've spoken to a lot of people out there who absolutely refuse to budge on their stance *'all kids go into care for a reason and social workers don't make mistakes.'*
Recently in the UK, a small child made headlines after he was killed by his parents. Social services missed vital signs of abuse and are being criticised for it. This is not the first time. We've seen several of these sickening incidents over the last few decades.
People are outraged at the social workers for this 'mistake' but those same people often seem to be totally unwilling to even comprehend that social workers make other kinds of mistakes, such as removing the wrong children for the wrong reason. They accept social workers mess up and cause death, but not that social workers mess up and cause family separation and adoption trauma.

People are quick to tell me I must have deserved it. I've even been told I am a conspiracy theorist. My lived experience is a hoax to many people and that's part of the problem with forced adoption; it's so unimaginably corrupt, people do not want to accept that they might be getting fooled on such a large scale. It makes us feel violated and stupid. We don't like that feeling, so it's natural to respond aggressively, the truth frightens people! We don't like our ideals challenged. We see this in politics, veganism, and religion all the time.

The problem is people do not ask the right questions. They are wholly focused on the birth mother and what she *'must have done.'* They never ask, how were social workers able to make medical choices for me? How was a social worker allowed to lie in court with no intervention? What did social services to do resolve the apparent issues before they proceeded to adoption?

Social services have people so convinced they are the good guys and that I am such a terrible mother, no one ever questions if they did enough, they only question if I deserved it. This is exactly the sort of behaviour West exhibits. It's the lasting fallout of emotional abuse.

If you read this book and still think my children and I deserved this, then far be it from me to argue with you. Thanks for your time, best of luck going forward.

It no longer matters to me what people think. I know what happened. This is my lived experience; a traumatic one I relive constantly. I know my faults and my strengths, and I am proud of how far I have come, how I survived my darkest days and finally developed the courage to tell the world my story.

Many other families out there are telling similar stories of their suffering with social services. There are many forced adoption advocacy groups and pages on social media and protests often taking place and yet, you probably didn't know that and won't do, unless it happens to you.

There was a time in my life I was against abortion and would never have believed social workers would take a baby for any reason other than physical or sexual abuse. I was wrong and I learnt that hardest way possible. Never take for granted your joy and never assume something about anyone. We all have stories, and we all deserve to tell them.

I urge any birth parents or adoptees reading this, who perhaps resonate with the agony within this book's pages, to consider writing or speaking their own story. I have found it deeply healing and my inner rage has ceased from raging pyre to flickering cottage fireplace.

I will never be ok. Even reunification with my eldest child has not stopped my grief. I still grieve the loss of the little boy I never got to watch grow up into the man he is now. The lasting impact adoption can have on everyone within the adoption triad is rarely considered during adoption proceedings and many families are not able to cope with the confusing emotions they are confronted with many years later when the kids' become adults.

There are many things in this book that should leave us asking questions about people in positions of authority in our social structure. We have many reasons as to why the adoption industry needs a reform and to start listening to adoptee voices rather than attempting to silence them and tell them they are being ungrateful when they want to seek answers about their birth origins.

Whatever your personal stance on adoption, the facts do not change, and the fact is, adoption often causes trauma and corrupt family court practices are now a root cause of adoption trauma and that root is destroying family trees.

Dear Leanne,

   Thank you for your
support + for sharing
your own story with me.
You are a brave soul

       Love.
          Lillian ♡

Printed in Great Britain
by Amazon